FASCISM:
THREE MAJOR REGIMES

MAJOR ISSUES IN HISTORY

Editor
C. WARREN HOLLISTER
University of California, Santa Barbara

Edward Chmielewski: *The Fall of the Russian Empire*

William F. Church: *The Impact of Absolutism in France: National Experience under Richelieu, Mazarin, and Louis XIV*

Robert O. Collins: *The Partition of Africa: Illusion or Necessity*

J. B. Conacher: *The Emergence of Parliamentary Democracy in Britain in the Nineteenth Century*

Basil Dmytryshyn: *Modernization of Russia Under Peter I and Catherine II*

Gerald D. Feldman: *German Imperialism, 1914–1918: The Development of A Historical Debate*

Frank J. Frost: *Democracy and the Athenians*

Paul Hauben: *The Spanish Inquisition*

Bennett D. Hill: *Church and State in the Middle Ages*

Boyd H. Hill: *The Rise of the First Reich: Germany in the Tenth Century*

C. Warren Hollister: *The Impact of the Norman Conquest*

C. Warren Hollister: *The Twelfth-Century Renaissance*

James C. Holt: *Magna Carta and the Idea of Liberty*

Thomas M. Jones: *The Becket Controversy*

Tom B. Jones: *The Sumerian Problem*

Jeffrey Kaplow: *France on the Eve of Revolution*

Archibald Lewis: *Islamic World and the West*

James T. C. Liu: *Major Issues in Traditional Chinese Political Institutions*

Wm. Roger Louis: *The Origins of the Second World War: A. J. P. Taylor and His Critics*

Heinz Lubasz: *Fascism: Three Major Regimes*

Leonard Marsak: *The Enlightenment*

Anthony Molho: *Social and Economic Foundations of the Italian Renaissance*

E. W. Monter: *European Witchcraft*

Donald Queller: *The Latin Conquest of Constantinople*

Joachim Remak: *The First World War: Causes, Conduct, Consequences*

Jeffry Russell: *Religious Dissent in the Middle Ages*

Max Salvadori: *European Liberalism*

W. M. Simon: *French Liberalism, 1789–1848*

Arthur J. Slavin: *Humanism, Reform, and Reformation*

W. Warren Wagar: *The Idea of Progress Since the Renaissance*

Bertie Wilkinson: *The Creation of Medieval Parliaments*

L. Pearce Williams: *Relativity Theory: Its Origins and Impact on Modern Thought*

Roger L. Williams: *The Commune of Paris, 1871*

Martin Wolfe: *The Economic Causes of Imperialism*

FASCISM:
THREE MAJOR REGIMES

EDITED BY

Heinz Lubasz

Department of History
University of Essex

John Wiley & Sons, Inc.
New York • London • Sydney • Toronto

Library of Congress Cataloging in Publication Data:
Lubasz, Heinz.
Fascism.

(Major issues in history)
Includes bibliographical references.
1. Fascism—Addresses, essays, lectures. 2. Italy
—Politics and government—1922–1945—Addresses, essays,
lectures. 3. Germany—Politics and government—1933–
1945—Addresses, essays, lectures. 4. Japan—Politics
and government—1912–1945—Addresses, essays, lectures.
I. Title.

D726.5.L8   909.82   72–8902
ISBN 0–471–55246–1
ISBN 0–471–55247–x (pbk.)

Printed in the United States of America

10 9 8 7 6 5 4 3 2 1

SERIES PREFACE

The reading program in a history survey course traditionally has consisted of a large two-volume textbook and, perhaps, a book of readings. This simple reading program requires few decisions and little imagination on the instructor's part, and tends to encourage in the student the virtue of careful memorization. Such programs are by no means things of the past, but they certainly do not represent the wave of the future.

The reading program in survey courses at many colleges and universities today is far more complex. At the risk of oversimplification, and allowing for many exceptions and overlaps, it can be divided into four categories: (1) textbook, (2) original source readings, (3) specialized historical essays and interpretive studies, and (4) historical problems.

After obtaining an overview of the course subject matter (textbook), sampling the original sources, and being exposed to selective examples of excellent modern historical writing (historical essays), the student can turn to the crucial task of weighing various possible interpretations of major historical issues. It is at this point that memory gives way to creative critical thought. The "problems approach," in other words, is the intellectual climax of a thoughtfully conceived reading program and is, indeed, the most characteristic of all approaches to historical pedagogy among the newer generation of college and university teachers.

The historical problems books currently available are many and varied. Why add to this information explosion? Because the Wiley Major Issues Series constitutes an endeavor to produce something new that will respond to pedagogical needs thus far unmet. First, it is a series of individual volumes—one per problem. Many good teachers would much prefer to select their own historical issues rather than be tied to an inflexible sequence of issues imposed by a publisher and bound together between two covers. Second, Wiley Major Issues Series is based on the idea of approaching the significant problems of history through a deft interweaving of primary sources and secondary analysis, fused together by the skill of a scholar-editor. It is felt that the essence of a historical issue cannot be satisfactorily probed either by placing a body of undigested source materials into the hands of inexperienced students or by limiting these students to the controversial literature of modern scholars who debate the meaning of sources the student never sees. This series approaches historical problems by exposing students to both the finest historical thinking on the issue and some of the evidence on which this thinking is based. This synthetic approach should prove

Series Preface

far more fruitful than either the raw-source approach or the exclusively second-hand approach, for it combines the advantages—and avoids the serious disadvantages—of both.

Finally, the editors of the individual volumes in the Major Issues Series have been chosen from among the ablest scholars in their fields. Rather than faceless referees, they are historians who know their issues from the inside and, in most instances, have themselves contributed significantly to the relevant scholarly literature. It has been the editorial policy of this series to permit the editor-scholars of the individual volumes the widest possible latitude both in formulating their topics and in organizing their materials. Their scholarly competence has been unquestioningly respected; they have been encouraged to approach the problems as they see fit. The titles and themes of the series volumes have been suggested in nearly every case by the scholar-editors themselves. The criteria have been (1) that the issue be of relevance to undergraduate lecture courses in history, and (2) that it be an issue which the scholar-editor knows thoroughly and in which he has done creative work. And, in general, the second criterion has been given precedence over the first. In short, the question "What are the significant historical issues today?" has been answered not by general editors or sales departments but by the scholar-teachers who are responsible for these volumes.

University of California   *C. Warren Hollister*
Santa Barbara

CONTENTS

Contents

FASCISM:
THREE MAJOR REGIMES

Introduction

The materials assembled here are intended to provide an introduction to the study of fascism. They relate to three important fascisms of the interwar period 1919–1945: Italian, German, and Japanese. The editor's aim is to present materials that allow the student to become acquainted with these fascisms both severally and comparatively. The selections have been arranged in rough chronological order, and by nation, because fascism has been at once an intensely historical and an intensely national phenomenon. But the selections can also be grouped into four topical rubrics for purposes of comparison: (1) those dealing with the "road to fascism" (Readings 1, 8, 21, and 22); (2) those bearing on ideological aspects of fascism (Readings 2, 5, 6, 9, 10, 23, 24, and 26); (3) those concerning the establishment of comprehensive power (Readings 3, 4, 11–13, and 25); and (4) those that exhibit or analyze the salient features of the fascist "New Order" in operation (Readings 7, 14–20, and 27). It is hoped that the student will thus see both what made each of these fascisms unique and what the common features were in virtue of which the label "fascist" came to be attached to all three. In this way he may appreciate some of the problems that historians and social scientists face in the study and analysis of fascism, including these vexed questions: (1) whether German Nazism did not go so far beyond Italian Fascism as to make the term "fascism" inapplicable to National Socialism; and (2) whether Japan was in any real sense fascist at all, given the great disparity between developments in Japan and developments in Italy and Germany. Additional materials on Nazi Germany have been included to allow the student to form an opinion on the first of these problems; a statement of the argument that Japan was not really fascist has been included (Reading 27) as shedding light on the second question.

It is not easy to say what fascism was, or is. Strictly speaking, the term "fascism" should be applied only to the movement, and then the regime, led by Benito Mussolini in Italy from 1919 to 1943. It was Mussolini who so named his own movement. Since no other similar movement or regime has precisely resembled Mussolini's, and since other movements have been known by different names—National Socialism in Germany, the Arrow Cross in Hungary, the Men of the Archangel in Romania, Falangism in Spain, to name a few—the label "fascism"—or rather "Fascism" —properly belongs to Mussolini's Italy alone. But there have indeed been other movements and regimes that have significantly resembled Fascism, and have consequently been labeled "fascist." The minor problem of distinguishing between Italian Fascism and similar movements or regimes can be solved by using the word with a capital F for Italy only, and with a small f for the others. That leaves only the major problem of establishing what the significant similarities are that justify the application of the label "fascist" to other movements and regimes.

Fascisms can be described and their histories written more easily than fascism can be defined. One eventually forms a general conception of what the disparate features are that have characterized fascist movements and regimes, but only after perusing the historical record at some length. To begin with a static definition of the sort that many social scientists like to work with —definitions cast largely in terms of institutions and structures —is almost certainly to place obstacles in the path of comprehension. This is so because fascism is characterized by a certain constellation of dynamic processes within specific historical settings, rather than by a definite set of specifically "fascist" institutions. The forms that fascism takes, the institutional structure it adopts, are directly related—as Mussolini recognized as early as 1932—to the specific national and historical context within which it arises. It is the dynamic of fascism that gives rise to its institutional forms, rather than vice versa.

A useful clue to the nature of this dynamic lies in its origins. Fascism came into being around 1919. The beginnings of fascism in Italy, Germany, and Japan are marked by the dual impact of World War I and the Bolshevik Revolution upon countries in which profound social and economic changes, long under way, were gravely straining the rather fragile political order, alarming the traditional elites, and threatening the situation of vast sections of the population at large. The chief threats were frequently perceived to stem from the capitalist powers—England, France, and the United States—and from the growing strength of the working-class and socialist Left. The former seemed to many people to have gained an unacceptable dominance through victory in World War I, the latter to have won a dangerous victory in the Russian Revolution. In this context, fascism presented itself as a political fighting force dedicated to the total defense of the nation against both the domination of the great *capitalist* powers without and the advance of *socialist* forces within. In due course, the fascist programs in all three countries, Italy, Germany, and Japan came to have this in common: they proposed to defend the nation against the external threat through a combination of autarchy at home and expansion abroad, and to stave off the internal threat by destroying socialism and setting up a rival "revolutionary" movement in its stead. Fascism proclaimed a political war on two fronts: against "Wall Street" *and* against "the Reds."

The fascist style can be characterized—too simply, perhaps, but not, I think, wrongly—as the introduction into politics of the ethos of combat. In this respect, too, the impact of World War I and of the Bolshevik Revolution was very great, perhaps decisive. Fascists exalted military virtues and the experience of a nation at total war: unity setting aside class and regional conflicts; unquestioned acceptance of directorial leadership; and collective commitment to a single, all-important, collective goal. The stance of the warrior, the language of combat, and the trappings of populist militarism were adapted to political life. Uniforms and parades abounded. So did paramilitary organizations. Every social, political, and economic task was portrayed as a struggle, a battle, a fight. Words such as "heroism," "honor," "loyalty," "obedience," and "leadership" were constantly bandied about. The whole world was transformed, in imagination, into fighters and their enemies. The future had to be "conquered." But, at least in Italy and Germany, the fascists also imitated the red revolutionaries. Acknowledging the power of Marxist ideology, they concocted "ideologies" of their own; recognizing the potential power of the masses, they formed mass organizations; sensing the widespread demand for fundamental social change, they gave themselves out to be revolutionaries (as a few actually were). All in all, mobilization was the keynote: mobilization military style, and mobilization revolutionary style.

But mobilization for what? The positive objectives of fascism were rarely clear. Indeed, when it first made its appearance, fascism was little more than a determination to do battle on the political front, to fight for "the nation" and against "the enemy." The first and principal enemy in Italy, Germany, and Japan was socialism. Even though fascism presented itself as hostile to capitalism as well as to socialism, nothing much ever came of the anticapitalism. Only the Nazis had the ingenuity to "discover" that international capitalism and international socialism were, at bottom, the same thing: two facets of one and the same phenomenon—the Jewish world-conspiracy. The Italians and the Japanese, having few or no Jews in their midst and no deep-rooted traditions of anti-Semitism to play on, were not able, as the Germans were, to substitute an assault on the Jews for the promised assault on capitalism. The assault on socialism was, in any case, serious and successful. It was eventually coupled with attacks, equally serious and often equally successful, on neighboring countries, preferably smaller and weaker than the homeland of the conquering herocs: Mussolini attacked Ethiopia and Albania; Hitler went, in turn, for Austria, Czechoslovakia, and Poland; and Japan invaded a decaying and desperately divided China. (It is curious how fascist "heroism" thrived on beating down the small, the weak, the defenseless; and how, when at last it tackled the giants—the United States and the U.S.S.R.—it collapsed in defeat.) This commitment to assault, this essentially negative, destructive commitment, characterized fascism from first to last.

What, then, of the positive side of fascism? In opposition to socialism, fascism promised to make a different and a better kind of revolution: a revolution that would unite the nation instead of dividing it along class lines, that would advance the interests of all, and that would restore the nation to its erstwhile imperial glory. It promised to make everything different, to make everything better. But because fascism had no practicable notions of how, in fact, to "make everything better;" because it needed the established economic and political elites; and because there was no way dramatically to improve the lot of peasants, workers, shopkeepers, clerks, or professional people without curbing the wealth and power of the privileged—wealth and power which the fascists wanted, in the last resort, not to destroy but to control— for these reasons fascism in power never made the revolution it had promised while it was merely a movement competing with socialism. It was often able to provide employment, to offer career opportunities, and to make available land for colonization and alien labor for exploitation. But these "positive" achievements depended entirely, and were wholly parasitic upon, the success of the negative commitment to destruction and conquest. When the commitment to aggression ended in military defeat, nothing positive was left of what fascism had built. Or almost nothing: Hitler's positive legacy to Germany was the *Autobahnen* and the *Volkswagen*. What survived the defeat of fascism in Italy, Germany, and Japan was precisely that set of social, economic and political problems that the fascists had promised, a generation earlier, to solve, but which, in fact, they merely bypassed.

If fascism made no revolution in the sense of undertaking the radical transformation of society, did it make a revolution in the sense of undertaking a revolutionary seizure of power? In Italy and Germany the seizure of power was largely a fake; in Japan it did not occur at all. Mussolini's "March on Rome" and Hitler's *Machtergreifung* (literally: seizure of power) were carried through with the benevolent neutrality or active cooperation of the army and police, facilitated by the intrigues of leading members of the existing establishment, and crowned with invitations by the respective heads of state—in Italy, by King Victor Emmanuel III; in Germany, by President Hindenburg—to form a government. Both Mussolini and Hitler were then granted extraconstitutional dictatorial powers. It was only when they had already been installed and furnished with authority that they proceeded to make full use of their positions to impose repressive, directorial rule upon their respective countries.

It has been so often said that fascism marched to power on the backs of the faceless masses who understand nothing of politics and care nothing for democracy that one is duty-bound to underline the significance of the following facts: (1) that neither Mussolini nor Hitler had the support of more than a minority of the population in any election preceding their respective acces-

sions to governmental power; (2) that the actions and policy pro-
nouncements of each were endowed with an aura of legality and
propriety by the very actions and attitudes of those sections of
the established elites that invited them to rule and handed them
dictatorial powers; and, (3) that in Japan fascism did not come
to power in the form of a movement "from below" at all, but
"from above." (Indeed, fascism in Japan was a matter of the
existing establishment's adopting fascist policies gradually and
piecemeal, and thus taking the wind out of the sails of what little
there was of a fascist movement.) It may well be that the old
elites did not quite realize what they were letting themselves in
for when they offered power to the fascists. It is true that the
fascists enjoyed some popular support. But it is a grave distortion
of the historical record to make "the masses" wholly, or even
principally, responsible for the rise of fascism. Yet this is the
view propounded by the so called "theory of mass society."

The theory of mass society seeks to explain the rise of fascism
in terms of the dysfunctions of a social structure composed of
masses and elites. It has been for some years now the dominant
theory in the United States for the analysis and explanation of
"totalitarianism" in general and of fascism in particular.[1] In a
very real sense it is an attempt to refute the older, Marxist theory
that explains the rise of fascism in terms of struggles within a
social structure composed of classes and dominated by capital.
These two theories, however, are not merely intellectual rivals:
they are also ideological antagonists. As surely as the Marxist
theory is tied to an apologia for the working class and for revolutionary politics, so the theory of mass society is intimately tied
to an apologia for elitism and for the politics of established orders.
The former sees fascism as the inevitable last gasp of capitalist
society in crisis; the latter sees it as part of the political pathology
of modern mass societies whose elites have lost authority. Neither
of these theories is without value. But neither is an adequate
explanation of fascism.

Neither of these fundamentally sociological theories of politics
will adequately explain the rise of fascism, if only because politi-

[1] The best known American treatments of fascism in terms of the theory
of mass society are Hannah Arendt, *The Origins of Totalitarianism*, Carl J.
Friedrich and Zbigniew Brzezinski, *Totalitarian Dictatorship and Autocracy*,
and William Kornhauser, *The Politics of Mass Society*.

cal actions and attitudes varied enormously *within* every segment of the social structure. Whether these segments be identified as classes, or as masses-and-elites, the fact is that all the classes were divided internally as were the masses and the elites. So, indeed, were individuals divided: the King of Italy was no fascist, and President Hindenburg was no admirer of ex-Corporal Hitler; yet both were eventually persuaded to admit the fascists to power. Nor was there anything inevitable about the fascists' accession to power, no matter how grave the social crisis. Hitler's movement, for instance, was not only in decline but on the verge of bankruptcy at the very moment when he was invited to become Chancellor.

There is more to the rise of fascism than sociological theory—"class" or "mass"—can explain. There is need for new ideas and fresh perspectives.

PART ONE

Italian Fascism

1 FROM

A. Rossi
The Rise of Italian Fascism

The Socialist and Communist Left, including the working class trade and labor unions, was the first principal target of fascist attacks, and was quick to see fascism as an enemy. Appropriately enough, the earliest definitions and analyses of fascism came from men on the Left. One of the most famous of these definitions was formulated in 1935 by the Communist Dimitroff, who saw fascism as "the openly terroristic dictatorship of the most reactionary, most chauvinistic and most imperialistic elements of Finance-Capital." The view that fascism is in fact the dictatorship of capitalism in its death throes, has had a long career and is by no means extinct. It follows, logically enough, from Marxist over-simplification of twentieth century conflicts into the struggle between socialism and capitalism, and between revolution and counterrevolution. Yet it fails in two crucial respects that are intimately connected: it fails to perceive the complex and elusive character of fascism and, as a result, fails to guide counteraction into effective directions. It also fails to evaluate adequately the errors of the Left that contributed to the rise of fascism. It is in this context that Rossi's analysis of the rise of Italian Fascism, written at about the same time as Dimitroff's definition, can most easily be seen for the remarkable piece of work it [is,] doing justice to the complexity of fascism and avoiding the simple

SOURCE. A. Rossi (Angelo Tasca), *The Rise of Italian Fascism, 1918–1922*, (London: Methuen and Co., Ltd., 1938; reprinted, New York: Howard Fertig, Inc., 1966), pp. 323–337. Reprinted by permission of the publishers.

11

Comintern view that fascism is simply the servant of big business or of finance capital. And, despite Rossi's own socialist convictions and commitments, it takes account of the failures of the Left.

When the post-war crisis began, Italian national unity had been established for barely fifty years, and the part played by the masses in winning it had been small. After 1870 the old oligarchies had only one aim in view: to suppress the fourth estate and deprive it of every means to direct action and power. On this point the conflicting forces of Vatican and monarchy were agreed. There were no democratic or revolutionary traditions, and the parliamentary system had remained an artificial improvisation grafted on to the life of the nation, whose growth had not been helped by the corrupt methods of Giolitti's reformism. The only really democratic force was the working-class and socialist movement, but this was handicapped by its narrow outlook and concentration on municipal affairs. Nevertheless the people—workers, artisans and peasants—with the traditions of their own independent institutions, were slowly making their weight felt in the state, when their progress was interrupted by the war. This was begun and carried on in Italy as a civil war, and coincided with a grave crisis in the ruling classes. The war was followed by depression and disorder: economic crisis in the country, which was exhausted and dislocated by the effort of victory; moral crisis among the people who, "while being and feeling victorious, were suffering the humiliation and crisis of the vanquished."

Within these wider causes there were other factors which helped to alter the course and the outcome of Italy's post-war history: the failure of the socialist movement; the reactionaries' and particularly the landowners' offensive in the form of military action and territorial conquest; the economic crisis of 1921; the help and complicity of the state and its dependent bodies; the discrediting of Parliament; the part played by Mussolini.

. . .

Most important were the socialist feebleness and mistakes, which were the direct cause, not of fascism itself, which appeared in every country after the war, but of its success in Italy. This becomes evident if one follows from day to day, as we have done, the policy of all the proletarian parties—socialist, maximalist, communist—in the years 1919–1922. It is helpful, though, to look still further into some of their failures and mistakes.

In so doing we may lay ourselves open to a charge of injustice towards the Italian working-class and socialist movement. But this is not the history of that movement, nor the biography of some of its leaders (Matteotti, Turati, Treves, to mention only those who are dead), whose moral greatness was sometimes actually a cause of political inferiority. Nor is this the valley of Jehoshaphat, where faults and merits are meticulously scrutinized. . . . We are combatants who accept, as they come, the tasks imposed on us by the time in which we live. It is our object to record the causes of a catastrophe where results have been grave in the extreme and will take long to repair. But we can only bear the responsibility for the past by a firm determination to avoid, so far as it is within our power, a recurrence of the same mistakes and the same disasters. Only candid and ruthless self-examination can give us the right to draw publicly the conclusions from our experience, and can transform our suffering into a message for others.

The fundamental weakness of Italian socialism in every sphere was due to its lack of true revolutionary spirit. This spirit is drawn by two allegiances: the refusal to accept the injustice, disorder and meanness of existing society, and the will to arrive at a new economic regime, new institutions, arising out of new relationships between men. Condemnation of the present must be enlightened, strengthened and justified by affirmation of the future. Only in this sense is there any truth in Bakunin's saying, "the passion for destruction is a creative passion." But it has been truly said of Italy that "hatred of everything old deadened even the desire for a new order," and that is why this hatred was so impotent.

For a class to be really revolutionary it must, says Marx, "first be aware that it is not a particular class, but the representative of the general needs of society." Italian socialism lacked this leaven, which alone could have raised it to victory. With a middle class crippled, clinging to its class point of view in the midst of the great upheaval which had intensified its egoism and its greed,

the socialist movement had a great part to play. If it had been
strong enough to remain faithful to it, it might have saved the
Italian people.

Instead it shirked its task. It lurked in the background all
through the post-war crisis. This desertion is the sole explanation
of the fascist success. Society, even more than nature, abhors a
vacuum, and the forces of barbarism are ever ready to rush in
and fill it.

The Italian socialists waited for the middle class to die off
naturally, without considering whether its death struggle, as they
assumed it to be, if unduly prolonged, might not generate seeds
of decay which would infect the whole nation, the socialist movement included. They behaved like the sole heir to an estate who
prefers not to turn up till the last minute, just before the will
is read. While they waited they confined their activities to "sep-
arating their own responsibilities from those of the ruling classes."
This separation was, up to a point, justified and even necessary.
But responsibility for evil committed is always shared by those
who have failed to prevent it; and we have no right to connive
at others' actions unless we are prepared to step in at the right
moment and succeed where they have failed. It is all the easier
to separate our own responsibilities from those of the ruling
classes if we are able and willing to shoulder our own responsibilities on behalf of an entire nation. If not, it is quite simple to
avoid "legal" responsibilities by pleading a kind of alibi, the last
resort of all scoundrels. ("Nothing like a alleybi" was the advice
given by Sam Weller's father to Pickwick.) In so doing we incur
a much heavier responsibility to history, whose judgments go
much deeper than any legal code. Useless, then, to say "We were
not there." The masses, who have lost all, will want to know why
not.

The policy of the Italian communists and maximalists was to
let things get as bad as possible. A policy which depends on ag-
gravating a situation the better to control and direct it is justifi-
able so long as one is ready and willing to intervene at the right
moment and restore order in the chaos that follows. Such tactics,
which must be employed with the utmost precision, become too
easily a game of chance, depending as they do on the blindest
and least reversible of forces.[1]

[1] The revolutionary defeatism of the bolsheviks in 1917 had an instantly

The Italian maximalists and communists had no idea of tactics: theirs was a state of mind that combined demagogy with inactivity and was quite devoid of the prophetic passion which calls down evil in order that virtue may triumph more brilliantly, and of the creative spirit which is capable of bringing about a vigorous transition from lowest to highest.

Such failings always imply a lack of humanity: the syndicate, section, party or class remains hidebound by its own limitations, and instead of regarding them as such, ends by making a fetish of them and loses that power of transcending them, which is the supreme necessity and spirit of socialism. This was the sole cause of the hiatus between the labour organizations, political and syndical, and the mass of the people.

Many of the socialist leaders thought that the vague popular movement which followed the armistice was just a "war psychosis." This was doubtless true, but it was not the whole truth. Those who fought in the war came in contact with the "system" and were swept up and controlled by it for four years. The war had torn them abruptly from their parish pump outlook and given them a stormy introduction to real politics. A whole generation was united in a common experience of an extraordinary nature. Afterwards the mass of ex-servicemen everywhere felt that they were on the threshold of a new life. They revolved vague, half-formulated ideas which led them to seek contact with each other and to feel conscious of the need to fight for their common salvation. As was to be expected after the shock and the bloodshed, their reactions were not always normal. But there was a real feeling that "we must not be taken in again," a feeling which ought to have been directed towards definite ends. Instead all that was noble and potentially humane in this emotional upheaval remained inarticulate, ignored, until finally it was exploited only to rescue from the past what had better been left there.

---

paralysing effect on the October revolution. For not only did Kerensky find it impossible to carry through the offensive measures demanded by the Allies, but Lenin too was unable to pass from defeatism to revolutionary war; hence Brest Litovsk. To-day it may be argued that this worked well, as the central powers were forced to quit the Baltic countries and the Ukraine, and Soviet Russia was saved in spite of all. But this resulted not from the military paralysis of the revolution at the beginning of 1918, but in spite of it, and from a combination of quite unexpected circumstances.

The socialist movement failed to realize how the war had thrown the great unorganized masses into the foreground. A movement on such a scale was beyond the old syndicate or party standard. The soldier back from the front found a society at once too unstable and too orderly for his liking. The revolution itself was too orderly—party card, syndicate subscription, membership of the co-operative, difficulties he could not get over, faced as he was by mistrust or tolerance, both equally insufferable. The Italian socialist leaders could no more understand the ex-servicemen of 1919–1920 than the German syndicates understood the unemployed of 1929–1932. Even Turati, so humane and so enlightened, felt that his chicks had turned into birds of prey. His socialism was a matter of conscience and education. In this he was right, but the time had come for the pedagogues, however noble, to give way to the prophets and missionaries. The sheltered flock in the party and the syndicates ought to have been neglected a little in favour of the lost sheep wandering in their thousands over waste land, so that they too could be saved.

Owing to the immense success of their co-operatives, Chambers of Labour, and town councils, the socialists of the Po valley believed they were simply going to absorb the old regime. Every day new institutions were growing up which to some extent foreshowed a society freed from the obsession of profit. But in legitimate pride in the results obtained they lost sight of their limitations, and socialism by remaining local and provincial became the victim of its own success. It went so far as to make a virtue of its faults. It was no longer only the old Italy, but socialism itself, the socialism of Reggio Emilia, which *farà da se*.[2] There was no point in considering the problem of the state, which supplied credits, grants and public works on demand. "Here," explained the socialist chiefs, "we are already in power. If the whole of Italy becomes a Reggio Emilia the revolution will be made." This "socialism in a single province" lost in breadth what it gained in depth; and breadth for socialism is not a matter of mere dimensions, but forms part of its very essence. The rate of its spread decides its nature and its destiny. Through its ignorance or neglect of the peasants of Apulia and the herdsmen of Sardinia

2 "Will act on its own," a phrase which appeared during the *Risorgimento*, expressing independence of outside help.

it lost contact with the nation and with the reality of socialism. It lost too the sound knowledge that none of its work would last while the "oases of socialism" were still isolated in a desert whose sands might at any moment submerge them. This kind of socialism not only fails to lead to revolution, but risks losing all its conquests, as it did in Italy. The real essence of local and gradual action is to keep in touch with the state on the one hand and to further the aims of socialism on the other. In the absence of this twofold outlet the political capacity, to use Proudhon's phrase, that the working class develops in its own institutions is lost to the community. The Italian socialists were utterly incapable of relating their ideals to the tasks imposed on them by circumstances.

Through this lack of perspective a prodigious quantity of devotion and human material, far superior to that behind many other political or religious movements, was wasted, and the chosen people, who had already arrived at the threshold of the new city, were disarmed and vanquished.

The socialists of the extreme left, on the other hand, invoked at every step their final aim of "proletarian revolution." On principle everything was sacrificed to this. For them there was no question as to whether their aim was consonant with the general interest; it was an accepted dogma, an historical fact, that it was so. Henceforward human emancipation was the work of the proletariat, and of the industrial proletariat in particular, acting through its leaders and its political party. And in their turn the party leaders became the trustees of the general interest and identified themselves with its progress and its demands. To look back and see if the sanctity of the apostolic succession had survived so many stages was pointless. There resulted a sectarian frame of mind dominated by a theological hatred of all who refused to recognize the divine quality of their mandate. So at the decisive moments in the Italian crisis the communists were fiercely opposed to a "united front," which they had never seriously or loyally supported.

The ideas and behaviour of the communists over the alliance of the proletariat with other social classes were characterized by the same sort of trickery. These were used as mere pawns in a strategy which was carried on over their heads. The alliance was not conceived of as depending on a common principle to which the proletariat and its allies were bound in equal measure. On the contrary "partial demands" were discussed, for the sake of an agreement that was only provisional and involved no deep or lasting obligations. While all goes well such differences pass unnoticed, but when the pace slackens the other classes begin to take notice and to claim their independence. This is what happened in Italy.

The alliance was founded on a very impermanent community of interests, and not on a desire for emancipation, which alone could have made it worth while or durable, and it ended not in mere disruption but in actual conflict. For the middle classes fell easy victims to manœuvres aimed at turning them against the proletariat. Fascism gave them an ideology which flattered their worst instincts by allowing them to believe that they were playing an independent and decisive part. The "arbitration" of the middle class between capitalists and workers was set up against the "hegemony" of the proletariat. One conception displaced another and the human raw material of the "revolution" was sacrificed to it.

. . .

The working-class and socialist movement in Italy was therefore defeated largely because, as Filippo Turati said, it was reduced to "teaching the proletariat to shirk at a time when the country was faced with the most urgent and burning problems." A graphical representation of the two movements would show them to be in some degree complementary. The socialist curve rises until the spring of 1920, when it fluctuates (defeat of the Turin general strike), hesitates, then rises suddenly with the factory occupations in September. Then there is a continuous fall till the march on Rome. The fascist movement, powerless until the early months of 1920, scarcely revived by the employers' great offensive which led to the occupations, rose steeply during the last three months of 1920 and continued to rise rapidly in 1921. The decline of the working-class and socialist movement was due entirely to internal causes, and preceded and made possible the victorious outbreak of fascism. In an article written at the end of 1920 Mussolini said: "In the past three months . . . the psychology of the Italian working class has changed profoundly," and on July 2, 1921, sixteen months before the march on Rome, Mussolini recorded: "To say that a bolshevist peril still exists in Italy is to accept a few disgraceful fears as the truth. Bolshevism is beaten." Mr. Bolton King, who has written the best history of the *Risorgimento*, has rightly come to the following conclusion:

"Fascism had no part in the Bolschevist collapse; it was as yet not strong enough to make itself felt effectively, and Mussolini indeed had smiled approvingly on the occupation of the factories. There is no substance in the myth that it saved Italy from Bolschevism. But the myth is a convenient one and it still lives in dark corners."

In Italy this myth has become the object of an official cult very useful for the purposes of the internal and foreign policy of the fascist regime. It is nevertheless true, however, that it was not fascism which defeated the revolution in Italy, but the defeat of the revolution which determined the rise and victory of fascism.

Why did fascism only begin really to take hold when its historical necessity, or as much as it had claimed for itself, had disappeared? Because the movement was not merely defensive, but a deliberate attempt to wipe out the forces and strongholds of the enemy. In this way alone could the privileged classes and especially the landowners attain their object, which was, not to restore equilibrium, but to profit by its destruction. The retreat of the enemy only whetted their appetite for reaction and revenge. When, for a few weeks towards the middle of 1921, Mussolini toyed with the idea of a general settlement on the basis of a compromise, the fascists in the country districts frustrated his plans and found support for their intransigence in all conservative centres. Aggressive fascism of the *squadrismo* type was born of the union of the capitalist offensive with the ambitions and appetites of various sections of the middle class, left by the ebbing of the tide of war which had carried them along nicely for four years. Thus, to borrow another expression from Turati, "a revolution in words," which had broken down after October 20, was followed by a "bloody counter-revolution," a "posthumous and preventive counter-revolution. . . ."

Just as the capitalist and fascist attack was being launched another factor began to weaken the workers' resistance. The slump became serious after the beginning of 1921, and the industrialists did not hesitate to use it as a weapon, proceeding to make whole-sale dismissals of their staffs. The workers' committees and syndicates began opposing them with their veto, but they could not hope to hold out long with purely passive resistance. The industrialists threatened to close the factories, and the workers no longer had any enthusiasm about occupying them. They tried compromise; with their strong sense of self-preservation and unity, the syndicates and internal factory committees imposed reductions in the hours of work of the whole staff, which they still had power to do, so as to avoid dismissals. This sacrifice by all for all considerably reduced wages all round. Those who were afraid of losing their jobs accepted this as a lesser evil, those who were or who believed themselves safe, eventually began to feel slightly uneasy and incapable of resistance. They became resigned to the elimination of one and then another category of workers: those who had a patch of ground in the sun, those who had no families dependent on them, the latest comers to the factory. This policy of despair gradually impaired the solidarity of the workers' front. Those who were sacrificed, with the tacit or formal consent of those who remained, departed embittered, sometimes desperate. Such a state of affairs could only be tolerated if it led to something better. But the workers, on the contrary, felt that they had reached an impasse, and that their sacrifice was useless, since anyhow the employers managed in the end to reduce their staff as much as they liked. The deadlock might have been ended by a firm policy uniting all the national resources to end the depression and assure at all events a minimum living wage to all workers. But who could have carried out such a policy? Not the socialists, who had been explaining for two years that this was a crisis of the capitalist system, that it was actually the final crisis of this system, and that the *bourgeoisie* must be left to shift for itself. Still less the ruling classes, whose one aim and obsession was the political and industrial enslavement of the workers. Fascism was there to simplify their task.

Consequently the slump, which the socialists had reckoned as an asset, proved their undoing. For every slump starts a process of social disintegration, with results that cannot be foretold dependent as they are upon uncertain human reactions. An exasperated desire to "put an end to things" somehow may lead to despondency and panic unless it is directed towards some concrete aim, and allowed a glimpse of a new order. The slump crushes those who cannot thus look ahead and are therefore without hope. Its value as a revolutionary factor lies in the forces of order it sets in motion; if these are not the forces of a new order, it only serves to consolidate the old.

. . .

The economic crisis in Italy coincided with a political one. Every branch of the state, police, executive, magistracy and army, gave its support to the fascists, in ways varying from tolerance to direct complicity. The ground was prepared for them, they were supplied with arms and transport, and they were promised immunity from punishment. Government decrees mouldered in files or were used exclusively against socialists. The government itself preferred not to be too deeply involved. For everybody was hoping to make use of fascism: Giolitti, to push the socialists into the government, the conservatives to keep them out, employers and landowners to liquidate working-class syndicalism, the monarchy and the Vatican to buttress the established order. They all relied on fascism as a temporary ally which could easily be disposed of later.[3] As matters stood, the state could only live a hand-to-mouth existence, going from compromise to compromise, from concession to concession. It had no source of strength. The mass of the people was estranged and hostile, and parliamentary crises followed one after the other continuously and without any signs of a solution appearing. Confusion, lassitude, and disgust, skilfully enhanced by controversy, and a kind of "planned defeatism" prepared public opinion for the justification of dictatorship. Liberty, in whose cause nobody, whether individual or

[3] We know how mistaken such calculations were. At the 1921 elections Giolitti got the fascists included in the lists of the "national bloc." When Count Sforza warned him of the danger of such a combination, he replied: "These fascist candidatures are nothing but fireworks; they will make a great deal of noise but nothing will come of it." The king shared the illusion, saying to Briand as late as December 1924 concerning fascism: "It is not serious, it will not last."

party, was prepared to sacrifice either ambitions or personal
wishes, was left defenceless. The threat to the state became a
threat to democracy.

. . .

In addition to the failure of the socialists, capitalist and fascist
aggression, the economic crisis, state complicity, and the breakdown of parliamentary institutions, there must be taken into
account the personal influence of Mussolini.

During the war he severed all that connected him with his
ancient beliefs. At heart, though, he had never been a real socialist. As a young man, consumed by pride and the desire to assert
himself, and obsessed by the idea that society was oppressing him,
he had broken away and taken refuge in Switzerland. As society
would not give him the position he wanted, his will to power took
the form of individual revolt. The experiences of his years of
exile had a decisive effect on him. Sometime he had been dependent for his daily bread on the help and goodwill of mere artisans
or simple decent socialists, or on petty dishonesty. Sometimes he
had had to take the roughest kind of work; he had fallen low,
and known extreme poverty. Such a life might have turned him
into a saint or a criminal, but he was too ambitious and too un-
scrupulous to take either way out. He learnt to set his teeth,
to calculate, to reject the romantic outlook and to grab his opportunity. Socialism could give him a start and serve for shelter.
In a few years he reached the highest position that the party could
give him, the editorship of its paper, *Avanti*. By the outbreak of
war socialism in its turn had become the obstacle that society had
been to him in the years 1900 to 1908. Mussolini did not hesitate
to break away a second time. After the armistice he realized that
he had to begin all over again and start a third struggle for
existence. From that time on his personal fortune is so closely
linked with the history of fascism as to be often indistinguishable.

If Mussolini had simply joined forces with the reactionaries in
1919 the flood would have passed over him and he would have
been left behind; he would not have found himself in March
supported by the ex-members of the "*Fasci* of Revolutionary Action" of 1914–1915, nor, a short time later, would he have managed
to collect a number of young men and ex-servicemen. Even if he

had formed the new *fasci* they would have perished with him. By the end of 1920 the situation had altered: the *squadristi* and the "slavedrivers," spreading from the valley of the Po, were advancing rapidly and overthrowing the socialist strongholds one after another. Mussolini hastened to make use of this movement, and revised his programme, declaring that "the reality of to-morrow will be capitalist." Towards the end of 1921 however, the movement was showing signs of getting out of hand and compromising his political plans. So he tried to frustrate it, denouncing its "greedy egoism which refuses any national conciliation"; he contrasted the "urban fascism" of Milan with the "agrarian fascism" of Bologna, "fascism of the first hour" with that which stood for the defence of "private interests and of the darkest, most sordid and most despicable classes now existing in Italy." Having announced in Florence: "Our programme is based on facts," he now clamoured for a "return to principles." A few months later still, when the situation had developed further, he trampled on the vague tendencies of Grandi and his friends towards "democracy" and "syndicalism," and from their opposition movement he took nothing but the bare principle of armed organization, stripped of any political significance; a simple weapon for the capture of power. Besides, although he disguised his plans in 1921 under a pretended "return to principles" Mussolini declared one year later that "to go back to the beginning, as some would have, that is to get back to the 1919 programme, is to give proof of childishness and senility." His versatility and complete lack of scruple proved an invaluable asset to fascism. It was he who prevented the attack on the Bonomi cabinet in autumn 1921; he who persuaded the group to support the Celli resolution in February 1922 (p. 174) and in July succeeded in preventing the formation of an anti-fascist group which might have become a government. If this had taken place fascism would have lost the support, or at least the connivance, of the state, and risked defeat. Finally, if Mussolini had not acted as he did, the march on Rome would have taken place in earnest and fascism would have met its doom.

Mussolini is not a genius; he merely has, as Mr. Bolton King so justly remarks, "the minor arts of a statesman." But these he possesses to a very high degree. Much of his strength has come from the weakness of his enemies. In 1919 he was simultaneously outbidding the demagogues and working for the cause of reaction.

This could never have happened if socialism had not allowed it. Faced with a constructive, which does not mean a watered-down Socialist Party, based on the traditions, institutions and powerful resources of the Italian working-class movement and free from delusions about soviets, Mussolini's tricks and manœuvres would have fallen flat. From the second half of 1921 up to the march on Rome Mussolini managed to exploit parliamentary action and *squadrismo* at the same time, thus, in Lenin's phrase, combining "legal with illegal action." But it was the socialist movement which gave him the necessary freedom of movement, by refraining from all action, legal or illegal, and thus delivering the country into the hands of its enemies. If it had been attacked through these inconsistencies fascism might have been crushed, but because they were neglected and allowed to flourish they became a direct cause of its strength and success.

The Italy of 1919–1922 lacked political leaders. Giolitti's mentality was pre-war, and when he returned to power in 1920 he was in his seventy-eighth year. The others, Nitti, Bonomi, Orlando, Salandra, all suffered from the same handicap: they were good scholars, but too academic to be able to deal properly with the post-war situation. The socialists had a few first-rate men, mostly on the right, but they were hampered by the conflict of doctrines inside the party and the working-class movement. The personal qualities of some of the communist leaders, such as Gramsci and Bordiga, could not outweigh the damage done by hopelessly wrong-headed tactics, and sometimes aggravated it. The maximalist socialists were a body without a head. Lamartine's description of a Girondin chief applied to most of their leaders: "One of those complaisant idols of which people make anything they wish except a man."

Italian socialism had need of a man, several men, in order to win, or, which came to the same thing, to avoid being wiped out. This was why Mussolini was able to reduce Italy to his own size and fill the entire horizon. With his advent the rule of "principle" came to an end, and his own personal adventure became that of Italy itself. For the better understanding of this crisis it is possible and indeed essential to trace back over centuries its remote and fundamental causes: the configuration of the land; the economic and social structure; the long enslavement of the people; the recent liberation, barely tolerated by some, barely assimilated by others. But these causes were not bound, inevitably, to lead to the events of the years 1919–1922 as they actually took place, with all their changes, their possibilities and their final result. New forces were growing up in Italy, alongside the prevalent lethargy, and for a certain space of time these balanced each other. In such cases momentary influences, including luck, may be decisive. The slightest variation may upset the balance and change the whole situation. Then it is that the actions of one man become of first importance, and history becomes a drama in which everything is linked up and nothing pre-determined, in which the epilogue may be changed up to the last minute, so long as the actors—individuals or groups—do not themselves rush towards the catastrophe. Contrary to a common belief, circumstances do not always of themselves create the men who are needed. Past history now provides a proof.

2   FROM

The First Program of the Fascist Movement
March 23, 1919

In its first program, the Italian Fascist movement presented itself to the public as progressive, republican, democratic, libertarian, peace loving, and anticapitalist. As the ensuing materials make plain, Fascism very quickly showed itself to be unprogressive, willing to compromise with monarchy, dictatorial, antilibertarian, imperialistic and not remotely anticapitalist.

1. A national Constituent Assembly, Italian section of the international Constituent Assembly of nations, which will proceed to a radical transformation of the political and economic foundations of collective life.

2. Proclamation of the Italian Republic. Decentralization of

SOURCE. E. Weber, *Varieties in Fascism.* Copyright © 1964 by Litton Educational Publishing, Inc. by permission of D. Van Nostrand Co.

executive power; autonomous administration of regions and municipalities by their own legislative bodies. Sovereignty of the people exercised by means of universal, equal and direct suffrage, by all citizens of both sexes, the people keeping the right of initiative for referendum and veto.

3. Abolition of the Senate. Suppression of political police. Election of magistrates independently of the executive power.

4. Suppression of all titles of nobility and orders of knighthood.

5. Suppression of compulsory military service.

6. Freedom of opinion, of conscience and of belief, freedom of association and of the press.

7. An educational system, general and professional, open to all.

8. A maximum of public health measures.

9. Suppression of limited liability companies and shareholding companies; suppression of all forms of speculation; supression of Banks and Stock Exchanges.

10. Census and taxation of private wealth. Confiscation of unproductive revenues.

11. Prohibition of child labor under the age of 16. Eight-hour day.

12. Reorganization of production according to the cooperative principle, including the workers' direct share of profits.

13. Abolition of secret diplomacy.

14. Foreign policy inspired by international solidarity and national independence within a Confederation of States.

3   FROM

The Memoirs of a Squadrist

Umberto Banchelli was typical of the fascist "legionnaires"
[squadrists] whose idea of political action was to carry out para-
military raids on workers and peasants, and whose idea of
economic reform was to beat up shopkeepers.

PUNITIVE EXPEDITIONS

"There was the expedition of S. Piero a Sieve, in which
Chiostri, Capanni (now Honorable Capanni), and Zamboni himself and Frullini participated—an expedition badly conceived
and badly executed. The *fascisti* fell into an ambush of peasants,
white bolsheviks. Bruno Frullini, giving the account of the expedition, tells how Zamboni and the other two fired like devils
at a closed window and did not stop until it was completely
shattered. From this it can be inferred that it was untrue that the
fascisti killed that peasant who was found dead behind a door-
way. . . .

In Tuscany our expeditions had spread terror in the camp of
the subversives. The Florentine *fascio* had gone as far north as
Carrara and as far south as Chiusi. Our squads were still in-
vincible even for the greatest vigilance of the reds.

The Hall of so-called Labor and the *Fiom*[1] had been entered,
their papers burned, and their banners taken. Red flags were dis-
played by the hundreds in the museum of the *fascio*. Communism
among the railroad workers received a mortal blow when Lava-
guini, its leader and perhaps the only one of all the red leaders
who was bonafide, was killed by an unknown person. The places
in town where railroad communists were well known to be in the

SOURCE. Herbert W. Schneider, *Making The Fascist State* (New York: Oxford University Press, 1928), Appendix (From the Memoirs of a Squadrist)
Umberto Banchelli, pp. 291–292, 294–296.

[1] *Federazione Italiana di Operai Mettallurgici.*

habit of meeting, were deserted *en masse* by these fathers of the revolution. For a long time there was no more talk of strikes. . . .

The countryside was searched daily: Empoli, Santa Croce sull' Arno, Fucecchio, San Miniato; then Perugia and the valley of Chiana. In that place there had been a communists' ambush, where several Aretine and two Florentine fascists were killed . . . barbarously assassinated but afterwards very fully avenged. It was a triumph of energy, though lacking the necessary discipline."

THE ECONOMIC QUESTION

"The more intelligent began to realize that the economic question was becoming more serious every day, and that the hour had come for launching labor syndicates. Fascism at that time was almost entirely unprovided with men competent in the field of economics; those whom they had, came from socialism and were caught in the general uncertainty. A few were not listened to. Others did not make themselves heard, because though being in evidence in fascist circles, they could not make up their minds to come out in the open and declare decisively what they thought. The cry went up that the worker must be befriended. Now at last they discovered how unfortunate had been the work of the young goody-goodies (*figli di papà*) who had erected an insurmountable wall over against the working classes. Perrone outdid himself in his efforts to succeed, but either because he lacked the necessary qualities or the suitable means, he could do little.

Now came a moment which was undoubtedly one of the most critical for our *fascio*. Caught between the duty of being the friend of the people, as had been said and re-said thousands of times, and the lamentable tears of the merchants, business men, and industrialists, from whom they had received money, our *fascio* preferred to do the noble thing and defend the people. However, the Directorate was not unanimous. The entire responsibility and direction of the hard work was entrusted to Banchelli in his capacity of Commissioner of Vigilance; the official rôle was entrusted to Pirelli. . . .

The desire of the Central Committee of *Fasci* was to defend the consumer and I observed this scrupulously. The campaign found me perfectly prepared. Scarcely had I been nominated Commissioner of Vigilance in the interests of civic police, when I had created a corps of 70 inspectors with about 1,200 men under them. To their previous duties was added that of reducing prices by the measures established. In a room in the *fascio's* office, I put a special tribunal and from it proceeded orders, inspectors, squads, punishments and praises. In order to avoid misunderstandings, before beginning the agitation and the cudgellings, I went out one day with a *centuria* of men, who carried large cards on which was written, "You have two days within which to reduce prices." We marched through the whole city amid the acclamations of citizens of all classes. In San Frediano (the poor district) the people wanted to carry us on their shoulders in triumph. Both out of political tact and in order to get closer to the mass of workers, we kept to the streets in which the people were thickest. Two days later, as predicted, the cudgellings began and prices were reduced in the just proportions, from fifteen to twenty-five per cent, established by the *fascio*. The cudgellings were innumerable, equal to the innumerable petty thefts on the part of the merchants. Whole squads, trembling from the blows received, were brought by the inspectors into the room of the tribunal to receive a little lecture of admonition, without partiality from all classes alike, from the currier to the wine merchant, from the clothing merchant to the broker. . . .

The egregious merchants of the town, instead of hating me, should have thanked me, for with the prices reduced they began to sell the merchandise which had been unsold on their shelves for three months. . . .

THE SARZANA EXPEDITION

"The Caporetto of Fascism." "About five hundred Tuscan *fascisti,* among them several fine ex-combatant figures, set out for Sarzana. Some of them were commanders of squads, but they were easily overruled by the undisciplined mob when the tragedy broke upon them.

The rendezvous was held in the country near the Avenza, and the march was started about two o'clock of the night of July 21st, under the light of a magnificent moon. In the minds of the *fascisti* there seemed to be something both mystic and grand about this column marching across the countryside! But an evil prophet thought it looked like a funeral march. This unfortunately proved to be true. As for tactics, we departed unorganized and unprepared for an emergency. The plan of action could not be read nor explained to the captains of squads, who moreover worried little about it, since in the matter of tactics almost all expected to use their own.

The idea was simple: to march upon Sarzana openly with one half of the force and in an orderly manner make the authorities surrender the nine prisoners; with the other half, if provoked, to ferret out thoroughly the squads of communists that were stationed in the environs of the city. . . .

Dumini, the leader, and his general staff had no choice but to march at the head of the enormous column marching single file, and to be the first to confront the communist ambush which reliable information gave us to understand was a certainty. The guides marched behind us. The march of sixteen kilometres carried us through the shadows and between farms and then along the railroad track. As a train was passing on its way to Sarzana undisciplined spirit made headway, and several shots were fired to halt the train. The leaders suppressed this impulsive conduct, but it was too late, for the railroad men spread the alarm at Sarzana.

The expedition was isolated from any friendly contacts. The few shots fired announced our march in advance, the aim of which could easily be imagined, and they proved a large factor in the staging of that tragedy.

At the inside gate of the Sarzana Station, two policemen begged the *fascisti* not to pass beyond them if they wanted to avoid being punished, and then as a compromise, we were told to pass by the side entrances, but the noisy mob broke out in undisciplined spirit, and insisted on doing the contrary. And so having passed on, about 200 of the *fascisti* reached a place where a police captain was stationed, one of Bonomi's hired assassins, together with eight policemen with their rifles in hand. They began a parley with Dumini and Santini, the captain of the Pisa squad. The parley was naturally interrupted by more than one of the *fascisti* present who also wanted to take part in it, until finally two pistol shots coming from the direction of the policemen immediately provoked a volley from the policemen's guns. It is worth noting that there were then two pistol shots, and also that the police captain suddenly raised his arm, with a stick in his hand,—a gesture which is commonly that of the commander of an executioner's squad. From the captain's manner of talking and his sarcastic smile at first quite indefinable, it was evident that he realized that we had witnessed something serious.

In fact the tragedy broke upon us unforeseen and like lightning. Our men had previously had strict orders that whatever happened at Sarzana no one was ever to fire at soldiers or at policemen or at Royal Guards, if there were any; so that very few of the *fascisti* answered the fire of the assassin policemen. What then took place was pitiful. Among the shots, the groans, the falling of the dead and wounded, there arose a general cry of indignation from many of those present. . . . The lack of moral and tactical unity provoked most of them to flight. In others it provoked bewilderment though they remained at their post under fire. A few retaliated. Among the many who fled into the countryside about thirty were wounded or killed in a truly barbaric fashion.

One need not go to Lybia to seek ferocity; the peasants of Sarzana gave such horrible evidence of their bloodthirsty rage that no revenge in the world could suffice to punish them adequately.

TOWARDS THE END

"Towards the end of September 1921, the directors of the *fascio* published the bombastic and rhetorical manifesto announcing that the *fascio* would retire from the struggle since the bourgeoisie was no longer giving it aid. It explained that fascism was being persecuted by the authorities with the consent of the democracy, and hence, its dignity being offended it would retire. . . . Really it was the directors[2] who were undergoing a crisis, for their personal ambitions had not been entirely satisfied! . . .

It is certain that the *fascio* of Florence for its own reasons did not want to be subordinated to any superior control. The crisis

[2] Rovello, Pelagratti, Pirelli.

had its origins far back in the very founding of the *fascio*, and all this because of the work of the moss-backed, slippered grey-beards. For from the beginning there were two policies and divergent aims: the market-place policy and the assembly policy, which together produced the bookkeeping policy. This was the logical consequence, and perhaps the only one, of Mussolini's giving fascism to Pasella to be wet-nursed.

It appeared at that time that between the *fascisti* of the *Partito Nazionale Fascista* and several autonomists, there would have to be some duels, but because of the gravity of the situation the disputes were pacified. Pasella and his Directorate continued to promote numerous subscriptions for all sorts of things, ever new sources of money. The expenses were always very heavy!—the rent of the new headquarters in Piazza Mentana is 18,000 *lire* annually. There were also, I believe, some lotteries and benefit entertainments, for the purpose of erecting marble memorial tablets. In a restaurant of the city, amid spaghetti and beefsteaks, they decorated with a gold medal one Mario Pelagatti, the friend from Spezia.

Pasella tried feverishly to win the sympathies of the workers and of the professional classes, in order to enlarge the little syndicates created by him and employed all the malcontents to swell the numbers.

According to my judgment, instead of democratic duels which never really settle any question, *fascisti* ought to wage duels *all' Americana,* or armed only with sticks. This latter is a better way also for the reason that the life of a fascist belongs entirely to fascism until the day of its complete triumph."

4 FROM   Christopher Seton-Watson
The Entrenchment of Fascist Dictatorship

The much-touted Fascist "March on Rome" on October 27, 1922, when some 26,000 ill-armed and ill-disciplined Fascist militants marched on the Italian capital, was no more a revolutionary "seizure of power" than was Hitler's appointment as Chancellor of the German Reich on January 30, 1933. The accession to power of the "Duce," like that of the "Führer" eleven years later, came through intrigue and was, in the end, offered on a silver platter— in Mussolini's case, by the King of Italy himself. In fact, on the great day of the "March on Rome," the Duce was not in Rome but in Milan, with a railway ticket to Switzerland in his pocket in case nothing came of the "storming" of the capital.

On October 30, the King asked Mussolini to form a cabinet, and on November 25, he granted him dictatorial powers until December 31, 1923 to establish law and order and to institute reforms. It was not until 1925–1926, however, that Mussolini, in the process of "clarifying the situation" created by continual Fascist violence against opponents of Fascism, suppressed all opposition and perfected the machinery of dictatorship.

Mussolini's promise to "clarify the situation within forty-eight hours" was not an idle one. The militia was mobilised, over one hundred members of the opposition were arrested, hundreds of homes were searched by the police and "subversive" groups dissolved. Prefects received orders to deal drastically with any expression of anti-fascism and to tighten their control over the press. Over the next two years the grip of the dictatorship steadily tightened and individual liberty dwindled. "We wish to make the nation fascist (*fascistizzare la nazione*)," Mussolini declared, "so that tomorrow Italian and Fascist will be the same thing."

SOURCE. Christopher Seton-Watson, *Italy from Liberalism to Fascism, 1870–1925* (London: Methuen & Co. Ltd., 1967), pp. 661–665. Reprinted by permission of the publisher.

"Everything in the State, nothing outside the State, nothing against the State" was his aim.

In February 1925 the extremist Farinacci was appointed secretary of the Fascist party, to the delight of the provincial *ras*. Though Federzoni was able, as Minister of Interior, to limit the amount of damage he could do, periodic outbursts of *squadrismo* continued. In October Florence was subjected to a night of systematic violence, arson, looting and terror. Meanwhile the judiciary lost the last shreds of independence. When the *squadristi* who had purged Molinella of socialism were acquitted on charges of murder and assault, Farinacci congratulated their judges on understanding the difference between crime and "an episode of the revolution." De Bono was acquitted by the High Court "for lack of evidence" and a week later was appointed Governor of Tripolitania. On 31 July an amnesty was declared for all political crimes except murder and manslaughter, and the penalties for these were reduced. In December the public prosecutor released all but five of the persons implicated in the death of Matteotti, on the grounds that it was a case of political abduction, not premeditated murder. Mussolini himself, writing in the fascist monthly *Gerarchia,* referred to "the involuntary character of what took place" and "a practical joke which degenerated into a horrible tragedy." In January 1926 the five accused were at last put on trial. Farinacci defended them "in Fascist style" and turned the trial into a prosecution of Matteotti and anti-fascism. Two were acquitted; the other three were sentenced to six years' imprisonment and under the terms of the amnesty released after two months.

The Aventine lingered on after January 1925. . . . In November the 123 opposition deputies, including the communists, were formally deprived of their seats. This was the Aventine's inglorious end.

Trade union liberty, like political liberty, was suppressed by stages. During the second half of 1924 the fascist syndicates organised a number of strikes, both agricultural and industrial, in northern Italy. One of their motives was to outbid the non-fascist unions for working-class support. In this they were unsuccessful. The socialists and communists, in spite of their divisions, were still far stronger than the fascists in industry. In March 1925 the fascists staged a limited strike in the engineering industry of

Lombardy, Piedmont and Liguria. The C.G.L. then intervened and greatly extended it, showing their power by keeping most of the strikers out for three days after the fascist syndicates had ordered a return to work. This was the last major strike in Italy for eighteen years. A month later the socialists and communists again won an overwhelming majority of the seats on the factory councils in the Turin Fiat works, and in July the Fiat management was forced to grant a wage increase. This was the last legal victory of organised labour.

On 2 October 1925 representatives of Confindustria and the General Confederation of Fascist Syndical Corporations met under the chairmanship of Farinacci at the Palazzo Vidoni, the party's headquarters in Rome. An agreement was signed by which the two organisations recognised each other as the sole legitimate representatives of workers and employers in industry. Rossoni, the fascist syndicalist leader, had at last reached his goal of a monopoly of organised labour. But the price paid was heavy. Over the next six months factory councils were abolished, chambers of labour were occupied by the police, strikes and lockouts were made illegal, wage contracts were given the force of law and machinery was set up for compulsory arbitration. While Confindustria remained intact in spirit, structure and personnel, the syndicates were subjected to an increasingly rigorous discipline under officials nominated by the Fascist party from above. Before long they had become mere cogs in the machinery of state. The Palazzo Vidoni pact was the death of genuine syndicalism. The non-fascist unions lingered on for a time, legally tolerated but powerless. "The remaining red and white organisations are destined to merge themselves [in the fascist syndicates] or to perish," Mussolini pronounced. They preferred to perish. The C.I.L. was dissolved in November 1926 and two months later the C.G.L. shared its fate.

Four attempts on Mussolini's life occurred between November 1925 and October 1926. Each was followed by violent retaliation against anti-fascists, in spite of orders to the contrary from Mussolini. Their effect was to create sympathy for him and to give the government the pretexts it needed for improving the machinery of dictatorship. After the plot of November 1925 by an ex-socialist deputy, Zaniboni, of which the police had been fully informed, the Unitary Socialist party was dissolved and the police occupied freemasons' lodges throughout Italy. The press was further restricted and Albertini was forced out of the editorship of the *Corriere della Sera* which he had built up to greatness. The servile parliament passed a series of "Fascist laws" for the defence of the regime which left the constitutional façade threadbare. These were the brainchild of Alfredo Rocco, ex-nationalist and leading theorist of the organic, collectivist, totalitarian state, whom Mussolini had appointed Minister of Justice in January 1925. Every kind of association was brought under state supervision and secret societies were made illegal—a law aimed in the first place at freemasonry. Three fascist commissioners were appointed to bring the ex-servicemen's organisations to heel. Judges, civil servants and teachers were subjected to a drastic purge and made liable to dismissal for activities or opinions "incompatible with the general political directives of the government." Mussolini was given the new title of Head of the Government and Prime Minister, to whom ministers were to be responsible and in whose hands the executive power was concentrated. The role of parliament was further reduced by the grant to the government of power to legislate by decree. The powers of prefects were increased, all the representative institutions of local government were swept away and 7,000 *podestà* were appointed to replace elected mayors of communes. Anti-fascists in exile, whose numbers were steadily growing, were made liable to loss of Italian citizenship and to confiscation of their property.

The machinery of dictatorship was perfected after the fourth attempt on Mussolini's life in October 1926. On this occassion blackshirt reprisals were on a savage scale. All parties except the Fascist were suppressed and the last remnants of an opposition press disappeared. All the communist leaders then in Italy were arrested and the badly disrupted party went underground. Gramsci disappeared into prison, to emerge eleven years later only to die. A thorough reorganisation of the police was carried out by its new chief, Arturo Bocchini, who was later to become one of the most powerful and efficient rulers of fascist Italy. The death penalty, abolished by Zanardelli's penal code of 1890, was reintroduced. The old penalty of banishment was revived and growing numbers of political opponents were sent to small islands or remote corners of Italy under police supervision. Emigration became illegal and passports were withdrawn. In January 1927 another law for the defence of the state made anti-fascist propaganda a treasonable offence and created a Special Tribunal for judging crimes against the state in secret. Twelve votes were cast against the law in the chamber, forty-nine in the senate. Shortly afterwards came the creation of a secret political police. The machinery of the police state was complete.

5 FROM *Mussolini*
The Doctrine of Fascism

To those who suppose that fascism was an attempt to implement a clear and specific vision of politics and society, it may come as a surprise to learn that until 1932—that is, until ten years after *the "March on Rome"—Italian Fascism had no official doctrine at all. The official doctrine was first formulated in an article in the* Enciclopedia Italiana *that appeared over the name of Benito Mussolini, though it was probably written by the philosopher Giovanni Gentile. The first section of the article appears below.*

(i) FUNDAMENTAL IDEAS

1. Like every sound political conception, Fascism is both practice and thought; action in which a doctrine is immanent, and a doctrine which, arising out of a given system of historical forces, remains embedded in them and works there from within. Hence it has a form correlative to the contingencies of place and time, but it has also a content of thought which raises it to a formula of truth in the higher level of the history of thought. In the world one does not act spiritually as a human will dominating other wills without a conception of the transient and particular reality under which it is necessary to act, and of the permanent

SOURCE. Michael Oakeshott, *The Social and Political Doctrines of Contemporary Europe* (New York: Cambridge University Press, 1942), pp. 164–168. Reprinted by permission of the publisher.

and universal reality in which the first has its being and its life. In order to know men it is necessary to know man; and in order to know man it is necessary to know reality and its laws. There is no concept of the State which is not fundamentally a concept of life: philosophy or intuition, a system of ideas which develops logically or is gathered up into a vision or into a faith, but which is always, at least virtually, an organic conception of the world.

2. Thus Fascism could not be understood in many of its practical manifestations as a party organization, as a system of education, as a discipline, if it were not always looked at in the light of its whole way of conceiving life, a spiritualized way. The world seen through Fascism is not this material world which appears on the surface, in which man is an individual separated from all others and standing by himself, and in which he is governed by a natural law that makes him instinctively live a life of selfish and momentary pleasure. The man of Fascism is an individual who is nation and fatherland, which is a moral law, binding together individuals and the generations into a tradition and a mission, suppressing the instinct for a life enclosed within the brief round of pleasure in order to restore within duty a higher life free from the limits of time and space: a life in which the individual, through the denial of himself, through the sacrifice of his own private interests, through death itself, realizes that completely spiritual existence in which his value as a man lies.

3. Therefore it is a spiritualized conception, itself the result of the general reaction of modern times against the flabby materialistic positivism of the nineteenth century. Anti-positivistic, but positive: not sceptical, nor agnostic, nor pessimistic, nor passively optimistic, as are, in general, the doctrines (all negative) that put the centre of life outside man, who with his free will can and must create his own world. Fascism desires an active man, one engaged in activity with all his energies: it desires a man virilely conscious of the difficulties that exist in action and ready to face them. It conceives of life as a struggle, considering that it behoves man to conquer for himself that life truly worthy of him, creating first of all in himself the instrument (physical, moral, intellectual) in order to construct it. Thus for the single individual, thus for the nation, thus for humanity. Hence the high value of culture in all its forms (art, religion, science), and the enormous importance of education. Hence also the essential value of work,

with which man conquers nature and creates the human world (economic, political, moral, intellectual).

4. This positive conception of life is clearly an ethical conception. It covers the whole of reality, not merely the human activity which controls it. No action can be divorced from moral judgement; there is nothing in the world which can be deprived of the value which belongs to everything in its relation to moral ends. Life, therefore, as conceived by the Fascist, is serious, austere, religious: the whole of it is poised in a world supported by the moral and responsible forces of the spirit. The Fascist disdains the "comfortable" life.

5. Fascism is a religious conception in which man is seen in his immanent relationship with a superior law and with an objective Will that transcends the particular individual and raises him to conscious membership of a spiritual society. Whoever has seen in the religious politics of the Fascist regime nothing but mere opportunism has not understood that Fascism besides being a system of government is also, and above all, a system of thought.

6. Fascism is an historical conception, in which man is what he is only in so far as he works with the spiritual process in which he finds himself, in the family or social group, in the nation and in the history in which all nations collaborate. From this follows the great value of tradition, in memories, in language, in customs, in the standards of social life. Outside history man is nothing. Consequently Fascism is opposed to all the individualistic abstractions of a materialistic nature like those of the eighteenth century; and it is opposed to all Jacobin utopias and innovations. It does not consider that "happiness" is possible upon earth, as it appeared to be in the desire of the economic literature of the eighteenth century, and hence it rejects all teleological theories according to which mankind would reach a definitive stabilized condition at a certain period in history. This implies putting oneself outside history and life, which is a continual change and coming to be. Politically, Fascism wishes to be a realistic doctrine; practically, it aspires to solve only the problems which arise historically of themselves and that of themselves find or suggest their own solution. To act among men, as to act in the natural world, it is necessary to enter into the process of reality and to master the already operating forces.

7. Against individualism, the Fascist conception is for the

State; and it is for the individual in so far as he coincides with the State, which is the conscience and universal will of man in his historical existence. It is opposed to classical Liberalism, which arose from the necessity of reacting against absolutism, and which brought its historical purpose to an end when the State was transformed into the conscience and will of the people. Liberalism denied the State in the interests of the particular individual; Fascism reaffirms the State as the true reality of the individual. And if liberty is to be the attribute of the real man, and not of that abstract puppet envisaged by individualistic Liberalism, Fascism is for liberty. And for the only liberty which can be a real thing, the liberty of the State and of the individual within the State. Therefore, for the Fascist, everything is in the State, and nothing human or spiritual exists, much less has value, outside the State. In this sense Fascism is totalitarian, and the Fascist State, the synthesis and unity of all values, interprets, develops and gives strength to the whole life of the people.

8. Outside the State there can be neither individuals nor groups (political parties, associations, syndicates, classes). Therefore Fascism is opposed to Socialism, which confines the movement of history within the class struggle and ignores the unity of classes established in one economic and moral reality in the State; and analogously it is opposed to class syndicalism. Fascism recognizes the real exigencies for which the socialist and syndicalist movement arose, but while recognizing them wishes to bring them under the control of the State and give them a purpose within the corporative system of interests reconciled within the unity of the State.

9. Individuals form classes according to the similarity of their interests, they form syndicates according to differentiated economic activities within these interests; but they form first, and above all, the State, which is not to be thought of numerically as the sum-total of individuals forming the majority of a nation. And consequently Fascism is opposed to Democracy, which equates the nation to the majority, lowering it to the level of that majority; nevertheless it is the purest form of democracy if the nation is conceived, as it should be, qualitatively and not quantitatively, as the most powerful idea (most powerful because most moral, most coherent, most true) which acts within the nation as the conscience and the will of a few, even of One, which ideal tends

to become active within the conscience and the will of all—that is to say, of all those who rightly constitute a nation by reason of nature, history or race, and have set out upon the same line of development and spiritual formation as one conscience and one sole will. Not a race,[1] nor a geographically determined region, but as a community historically perpetuating itself, a multitude unified by a single idea, which is the will to existence and to power: consciousness of itself, personality.

10. This higher personality is truly the nation in so far as it is the State. It is not the nation that generates the State, as according to the old naturalistic concept which served as the basis of the political theories of the national States of the nineteenth century. Rather the nation is created by the State, which gives to the people, conscious of its own moral unity, a will and therefore an effective existence. The right of a nation to independence derives not from a literary and ideal consciousness of its own being, still less from a more or less unconscious and inert acceptance of a *de facto* situation, but from an active consciousness, from a political will in action and ready to demonstrate its own rights: that is to say, from a state already coming into being. The State, in fact, as the universal ethical will, is the creator of right.

11. The nation as the State is an ethical reality which exists and lives in so far as it develops. To arrest its development is to kill it. Therefore the State is not only the authority which governs and gives the form of laws and the value of spiritual life to the wills of individuals, but it is also a power that makes its will felt abroad, making it known and respected, in other words, demonstrating the fact of its universality in all the necessary directions of its development. It is consequently organization and expansion, at least virtually. Thus it can be likened to the human will which knows no limits to its development and realizes itself in testing its own limitlessness.

12. The Fascist State, the highest and most powerful form of personality, is a force, but a spiritual force, which takes over all the forms of the moral and intellectual life of man. It cannot therefore confine itself simply to the functions of order and super-

---

[1] "Race; it is an emotion, not a reality; ninety-five per cent of it is emotion." Mussolini.

vision as Liberalism desired. It is not simply a mechanism which limits the sphere of the supposed liberties of the individual. It is the form, the inner standard and the discipline of the whole person; it saturates the will as well as the intelligence. Its principle, the central inspiration of the human personality living in the civil community, pierces into the depths and makes its home in the heart of the man of action as well as of the thinker, of the artist as well as of the scientist: it is the soul of the soul.

13. Fascism, in short, is not only the giver of laws and the founder of institutions, but the educator and promoter of spiritual life. It wants to remake, not the forms of human life, but its content, man, character, faith. And to this end it requires discipline and authority that can enter into the spirits of men and there govern unopposed. Its sign, therefore, is the Lictors' rods, the symbol of unity, of strength and justice.

6 FROM *Edward R. Tannenbaum*
The Goals of Italian Fascism

Professor Tannenbaum's essay is concerned, as its title indicates, with the aims rather than the achievements of Italian Fascism. But it does make clear, if only incidentally, that none of the goals was in fact achieved. The Italians were only the first among fascists in many countries who, though some of them may have been would-be revolutionists, made no revolutions.

The purpose of this essay is to discover what the Italian Fascists *wanted,* not what they did or who supported them. Any explanation of their rise to power would have to include the nature of the Italian crisis during and immediately after the First World War, the ways in which the ruling circles and opposition parties abdicated their responsibilities in the face of this crisis,

SOURCE. Reprinted from *The Fascist Experience: Italian Society and Culture, 1922–1945* by Edward R. Tannenbaum. Copyright 1972. By special permission of the author and Basic Books, Inc. Publishers, New York.

and, finally, Mussolini's tactical ability. Most people who accepted Mussolini at first were interested in the restoration of law and order, not in squadrism, syndicalism, or demagogic nationalism. By the mid-1920's his regime adopted much of the authoritarian program of the prewar Italian Nationalist Association, with which the Fascist party had merged in 1923. Although each of these two movements already had its own internal divisions, their fusion engendered the most acrid arguments over ideology between the half-educated former *squadristi* leaders who had made the "Revolution" of 1919–1922 and the nationalist intellectuals who tried to use this "Revolution for their own ends thereafter. There was also a conflict of generations here: aside from Mussolini himself most Fascist ras were still in their twenties when he gained power, and they resented the apparently preponderant influence of the older nationalists, especially Luigi Federzoni and Alfredo Rocco, soon thereafter. The Fascist syndicalists had wanted a new, autonomous labor movement, not the absorption of the workers into corporations dominated by the employers and controlled by the state. The *squadristi* had wanted the triumph of rebellious youth over the existing order and the older generation in all the other parties, not a bureaucratic Fascist party machine stripped of its political power. For many of them Fascism continued to mean beating people with a big club (affectionately called the *santo manganello*) and performing daredevil feats of courage.

The diverse goals of the Fascists have been obscured by the public behavior of their *Duce*. This is unfortunate, for the black-shirted *squadristi* were the first and most notorious example of one recurring form of youthful revolt against self-righteous liberal establishments. (Today's Hell's Angels motorcycle gang, with its black leather jackets, typifies this kind of revolt better than the white-hooded Ku Klux Klan, which is temperamentally reactionary.) Like Hitler, Mussolini had first expressed his disgust for the prevailing order before the First World War, but whereas Hitler got his initial ideological orientation from reactionary anti-Semites like Georg von Schönerer, Mussolini claimed to have been a disciple of Georges Sorel. The importance of these "influences" should not be exaggerated, but the fact remains that Hitler had never been a man of the Left, and he never attracted as many Left-wing revolutionary followers as Mussolini did.

Once in power Mussolini found it politically expedient to maintain much of the old order against which he had been advocating one form of revolution or another for over two decades. He certainly was opportunistic in his compromises with the monarchy, the state administration, the army, the big industrialists and landowners, and the Church. Yet even he never lost his hostility toward these groups or his desire to downgrade them in some way. Nor was he the only dictator who sacrificed ideology to state policy.

In contrast to Nazism, Fascism, at least in the beginning, had tried to present itself as a revolutionary alternative to Marxism rather than a mindless reaction against it. The founders of the Fascist movement in March 1919 were almost all former revolutionary socialists and syndicalists who by late 1914 had organized Fasci for Revolutionary Action urging intervention in the war. Their 1919 program was anticapitalist, antimonarchical, anticlerical, antisocialist, antiparliamentary, and, most especially, antibourgeois; they wanted to overthrow the existing establishment and replace it with a rather vague national syndicalist utopia. At first Mussolini viewed himself as a kind of Italian Lenin, with a desire to continue the war with a revolution.

By 1921, however, the original character of the movement had changed radically. As the fruits of victory turned sour, and as the liberal regime seemed powerless to control profiteers and strikers, many inexperienced, alienated students and younger veterans developed a "lost generation" complex and joined the Fascists in order to sweep away the sordid "mess" around them and to build a purer, nobler order. Beginning in late 1920 the rural *squadristi* in the Po Valley gave the movement an increasingly violent stance. These young rowdies introduced a distinctly provincial and anarchic quality to Fascism, specializing in vicious "punitive raids" against socialist and Catholic labor unions and the headquarters of rival parties. Many *squadristi* leaders accepted subsidies from the big landowners and businessmen, but they did not abandon their ultimate goal of making their own revolution.

After the Fascist regime was established, party spokesmen continued to expound divergent views about its nature and goals. Aside from glorification of the *Duce* and the nation the only slogan that most of them seemed to accept was the "continuing revolution." The public was told that the refusal of the regime to be imprisoned by a particular idea was a sign of its "living force, that is to say its validity as truth." But Fascist ideologues of both the Left and the Right interpreted the "continuing revolution" in several different ways. Edmondo Rossoni, president of the National Confederation of Fascist Unions during the mid-1920's, wanted Fascist syndicalism to be an effective champion of Italian labor against selfish employers. Roberto Farinacci, still firmly entrenched as the ras in Cremona after his dismissal as national party secretary in March 1926, continued to appeal for a resumption of squadrism. Giuseppe Bottai, Minister of Corporations and then Minister of Education in the 1930's, wanted new technical and cultural elites; he and his colleagues on the review *Critica fascista* urged the modernization of all aspects of Italian life. The reactionary nationalist Alfredo Rocco advocated, on the other hand, a constitutional corporate state.

It is obviously not to Mussolini, then, that we must turn for an understanding of Fascist goals but to those party ideologues who tried to push him in one direction or another. Until his dictatorship was firmly secure, he had considered the party as merely the military instrument for achieving his own personal power; thereafter he continued to view it with a mixture of suspicion and contempt. It was natural that the revolutionary activists who had participated in the march on Rome should have wanted to base the new Fascist order on their mode of organized violence and on an omnipotent but decentralized party oligarchy. In order to counteract this tendency (as well as to placate the conservatives) Mussolini temporarily enlisted the services and ideas of those nationalist converts to Fascism who preached the primacy of the state and its law enforcement agencies. The victory of Federzoni as Minister of the Interior over Farinacci as party secretary by early 1926 is well known, as are Mussolini's efforts to exploit the prestige of the philosopher Giovanni Gentile by adopting phrases like the "ethical state." Most important of all was the *Duce*'s decision to allow Rocco to create the constitutional facade of a "corporate state." Mussolini had no faith in trade-union leaders, technocrats, intellectuals, or any other kind of elite, yet he humored syndicalists like Pietro Capoferri as well as champions of a "managerial revolution," especially the editors of *Critica fascista*. He con-

tinued to tolerate such heterodoxy not only because of his opportunism and his diffidence toward the party but also because
he simply preferred to avoid open confrontations. . . .

While the rank and file of the *squadristi* were little more than
patriotic young gangsters, their leaders wanted a revolution that
would give them a monopoly of power; in order to achieve this
goal they first had to defeat the local forces of the Left. Only
after they already controlled a number of important local governments, at least in the North, could they hope to challenge the
central government itself. Hence, in 1921–1922, their "Revolution" took the form of a series of local civil wars in which their
victims were almost invariably the workers' organizations, both
urban and rural. Some union and Left-wing party leaders had
been trying to make their own revolution since 1919, but even
on the local level they were divided and poorly organized. The
"occupation of the factories" in September 1920 had frightened
the propertied classes without advancing the cause of the workers;
the ambition of certain Socialists, especially in Emilia, to "build
socialism in one province" had been equally unsuccessful; the
internal quarrels within the Socialist party and the Communist
secession from it at the Livorno Congress in January 1921 de-
moralized the workers at the very moment when the Fascists and
their reactionary backers were mobilizing their strength. Yet it
would be wrong to view *squadristi* violence and strike-breaking
activities merely as a reaction against the Red Scare. Balbo,
Farinacci, Ricci, and other leading ras used these tactics as a
means of making themselves dictators in their own provinces. . . .

The methods of many leading ras were as brutal as those of
Al Capone, but these men were not ordinary gangsters. They
wanted their gangs to take over the whole country, punish all
those citizens whom they considered subversive, and indoctrinate
the rest with a superpatriotic military spirit. Balbo's famous comparison between the activities of the *squadristi* and the Albigen-
sian Crusade was not merely high-flown rhetoric. The main
difference—and it was crucial—between the *squadristi* and the
northern French crusaders was that the latter were aristocrats in
the service of the King, whereas the former were plebeians trying
to destroy the legitimate regime as well as root out subversives.
Hence the *squadristi* were revolutionaries in a way that Capone
and Simon de Montfort were not, despite the common element

of brutality. Their revolution, however, was to be political; the old ruling groups were to be displaced by a new rough-and-ready elite, but the economic and social structures were not to be altered.

The *squadristi,* like all other Fascists, argued that they were making a "spiritual" rather than a materialist revolution, but since Mussolini stripped them of their remaining political power after 1925 they never had the chance to prove their case. . . .

Although the *squadristi* could not have realized their youthful ideal of regenerating Italy's "sick society" either with or without Mussolini, they did give Fascism its heroic, revolutionary, D'Annunzian stance. Mussolini himself openly assumed this posture in early August 1924 when he said that all true Fascists should be proud to reach their goals unadorned by titles and honorific trappings (*arrivare nudi alla mèta*) and that their motto should be: Live dangerously (*vivere pericolosamente*). The *squadristi* marching song, "Giovinezza, Giovinezza," which became the second national anthem along with the "Marcia Reale," vaunted bomb throwing and dagger wielding as well as youth as the springtime of beauty. Violence, youthful dreams, and blustering heroics were not unique to Fascism; they had a long tradition in Italy, and the *squadristi* openly borrowed much of their ritual, including the battle cry *me ne frego,* from Gabriele D'Annunzio's Fiume legions. The point is that many of them took these things quite seriously. Just as the goals of militarism are the glorification of the military way of life and its imposition on the state and the civilian population, so the goals of squadrism were the glorification of its way of life and its imposition on the state and the civilian population. The fact that the *squadristi* also thought of themselves as revolutionary activists gave them a mystique that the regime preserved—albeit as mere rhetoric—long after they themselves were either tamed or purged.

Whereas the ideal of the *squadristi* was a demagogic, gangster-like form of militarism, the goal of the militant Fascist trade-union leaders were a heretical version of revolutionary syndicalism. . . .

Beginning in 1925 Mussolini's regime instituted its own form of *Gleichschaltung.* As in Nazi Germany eight years later, this process involved the elimination of the opposition political parties and independent labor unions and the "coordination" of

the press, the schools, the courts, and other public agencies. Unlike its counterpart in Nazi Germany it also included the sub-
ordination to the state of the party itself and the organizations
it sponsored: militia, Balilla, *Dopolavoro,* and so forth. Mussolini
strengthened the faltering state administration he inherited,
especially the Ministry of the Interior; in Germany friction
between Nazi party organizations and the traditionally strong
state administration weakened the latter. Martin Bormann had
far more discretionary powers than any Fascist party secretary;
Robert Ley's Labor Front was able to challenge the *Reichsbank,*
the Ministry of Economics, and the party hierarchy itself, whereas
the Fascist unions and corporations could put no real pressure
on anyone except the workers. Yet despite the Fascists' subordina-
tion of other agencies to the state, their attempt to create a
totalitarian regime had less success than that of the Nazis. One
reason was that Mussolini never completely eliminated the influence of the King and the Pope; another reason was that, unlike
Hitler, he delegated the task of his *Gleichschaltung* to men whose
outlook was quite different from his: Federzoni (Minister of the
Interior, 1924–1926), Rocco (Minister of Justice, 1925–1932), and
Arturo Bocchini (Chief of Police, 1925–1940).

Of these three men it is Rocco who interests us here, since he
became known as "the official theorist of Fascism." . . .

Rocco's so-called corporatism was neomercantilist. Unlike Maur-
ras, he disapproved of autonomous intermediary organizations
like corporations, communes, estates, and the like. For Rocco,
"nothing outside the state" in the economic sphere meant neither
state socialism nor state capitalism; it meant the reorganization
of big business in a way that would avoid "useless internal competition in order to face, under conditions of maximum economic
efficiency, the battles of international competition." Rocco wanted
to eliminate all working-class autonomy, privileges, and influence
in productive enterprises, especially those gains made in 1919 and
1920. Unlike Saint-Simon, Rocco did not believe in the possibility
of harmony among classes. Defending strict state control over
his "mixed unions" of employers and workers against Lanzillo's
criticism, Rocco told the Chamber of Deputies: "The State, least
of all the Fascist State, cannot permit the constitution of States
within the State. The organization [in the 1926 laws] of the
unions must be a means of disciplining the unions, not a means

of creating strong, uncontrolled organisms capable of undermining the State." In one of his last public speeches he said that, in contrast to the medieval corporation, the Fascist corporation achieves a high level of discipline in the productive process not only in the interests of the producers

"but above all in the general interest, under the effective tutelage of the State. . . . Utilizing its technical competence and the stimulus of the individual interests of the producers it operates above all to make the production and hence the wealth of the Nation more perfect, more profitable, more considerable."

In other words, "What's good for General Motors is good for the country."

Rocco never saw his neomercantilist dream realized, partly because of the resistance of big business to state interference, partly because the depression halted the kind of juridical reforms he wanted, and partly because his economic and social goals interested neither Mussolini nor most other Fascists. The so-called corporate state that was finally achieved on paper in 1934 changed nothing; it merely continued the practices established in the 1926 laws disciplining labor without controlling management. It was his political goals, most of which *were* achieved in laws devised by him between 1925 and 1932, that made Rocco the "official theorist" of Mussolini's variety of Fascism.

These laws reinforced the *Duce*'s dictatorial powers by allowing him to legislate by decree, by outlawing all other political parties, by eliminating the possibility of subversion, by "demoting" the Fascist party from an autonomous "private" organization to a propaganda agency of the government, and by making the Fascist Grand Council Mussolini's "general staff." Even the government itself was reduced to the status of a merely consultative and executive organ without joint responsibility for decisions taken by its head. Increasingly, especially after the law of December 9, 1928, defining its organization and powers, the Grand Council became the highest deliberative organ of the regime. Not only was its approval necessary for all further constitutional changes; it also prepared the lists of deputies to be elected and union leaders to be appointed and was even empowered to rule on the succession to the throne and to choose Mussolini's eventual successor.

Mussolini and most party leaders lauded Rocco's concentration of all political power in the hands of the *Duce* and the Grand Council, but Rocco had envisioned a different kind of elite from the one that actually ran the Fascist regime from the early 1930's until its final demise. When Rocco left the Ministry of Justice in 1932 most of Mussolini's ablest collaborators were dismissed as well, including Giuseppe Volpi as Minister of Finance, Dino Grandi as Minister of Foreign Affairs, Giuseppe Bottai as Minister of Corporations, and Balbino Giuliano as Minister of Education. Thereafter the leading government ministers were mainly party hacks, although Bottai returned to office as Minister of Education in 1936. Rocco had wanted an elite of highly competent civil servants, progressive industrial tycoons, and "Solons" like himself. Instead the leading figures of the regime after 1932 were "tamed" former *squadristi* like Achille Starace, Renato Ricci, Ettore Muty, and Carlo Scorza. These and other untutored *gerarchi* flanking the *Duce* on all public occasions became the image of the Fascist elite for most Italians.

The inability of Fascism to produce a capable new ruling elite prevented it from realizing any of its diverse goals. Even Mussolini himself, despite his undeniable qualities of leadership and attraction for the masses, did not have the intelligence or character of a truly great and creative statesman. One of his most astute colleagues compared him to "an electric power station that illuminated one small lamp bulb . . . an energy that dispersed itself and evaporated for want of collecting centers, of links that might articulate it." In Weberian language Fascism was an authoritarian dictatorship in which the charisma of the leader did not become bureaucratized. This failure was due in part to the compromises Mussolini had to make with the older elites— monarchy, Vatican, army, state administration, big business— all of which endured alongside of the new hierarchical party organizations. It was also the result of his inability to reconcile his mania for making all political decisions himself with his growing indulgence toward the proliferation of rival administrative structures. Shorn of real political initiative, the party *gerarchi* were not forced to work out a unified ideology that they could hope to impose on the older elites and the masses.

Before concluding with some of the ideological efforts to revive the "continuing revolution" within the framework of the bureaucratized regime during the 1930's, we must dispose of Gentile's conception of the "ethical state." This conception served more as the wishful thinking than as the working ideology of Fascism, but it must be mentioned briefly because Mussolini himself followed it almost literally in his famous article on "Fascism" in the 1932 edition of the *Enciclopedia italiana.* The controversy over whether or not Gentile ghost-wrote this article is unimportant here. Certainly the first part, "Dottrina-idee fondamentali," is borrowed completely from Gentile's 1925 essay *Che cosa è il fascismo.* The second part, "Dottrina politica e sociale," diverges from Gentile in its emphasis on militarism, in its conception of the state as an entity independent of its citizens, and in its identification of the Fascist state with the Roman tradition. Gentile, of course, was the editor in chief of the encyclopedia, but it is unlikely that he edited Mussolini.

The first part of Mussolini's article assumes the basic premise of Gentile's "actual idealism": the identity of thought and action. From this premise Mussolini postulates the idea of an authentic community which Fascism is trying to make actual by fusing the individual and the nation. Only in such a community can the individual realize his true potentialities, which are spiritual rather than material, social rather than individual. The means for making this ideal a reality is the totalitarian state.

"Fascism reaffirms the state as the true reality of the individual. . . . For the Fascist everything is in the state, and nothing human or spiritual exists, much less has value, outside the state. In this sense Fascism is totalitarian, and the Fascist state, which is the synthesis and unity of all values, interprets, develops, and brings out the full potential of the total life of the people."

Thus the Fascist state is an *ethical* state because it alone makes possible the realization of true human values. "The nation as state is an ethical reality that exists and lives as long as it develops."

Mussolini liked Gentile's idea that the Fascist regime was the means of creating a new type of Italian and a new civilization. According to Gentile, the spiritual essence of Fascism, its "religious, totalitarian view of life," must inform the consciousness of all citizens and permeate every sphere of daily life. The idealist philosopher maintained that "politics and history are made not only by promulgating new laws, creating new institutions, or winning battles, but also (and properly so) by developing new states of mind, and ideas, in forming new men and a new spirit." Fascism for him was neither a philosophy nor a dogma; it was, rather, a "continuing revolution" of the immanent spirit of the nation. It was bound by no irrevocable policies: "The true resolutions of the Duce are those that are both formulated and put into actual effect."

This kind of language obviously flattered Mussolini, but he had no intention of making Gentile his Plato. First of all, he could not accept Gentile's idea that the state exists in so far as the citizens cause it to exist; for Mussolini and for all other leading Fascists, the state was autonomous. Furthermore, the "continuing revolution" was obviously over by the time of the Lateran Treaty. By then Gentile, who had been Mussolini's first Minister of Education and had headed an important constitutional commission, was relegated to purely academic posts and had no further influence on governmental policy. The hostility of the Vatican also made it necessary to downgrade him in Fascist circles. He was, in addition, attacked by many party officials for harboring anti-Fascist professors on the editorial board of his encyclopedia. Thus, by the time Mussolini's· article appeared in 1932 the man and the philosophy that had inspired it were already out of fashion.

In 1932 the "Fascist Revolution" was merely history and was enshrined in a public exhibition (*Mostra della Rivoluzione Facista*) on the Via Nazionale in Rome. This exhibition depicted the events of 1919–1922, stressing the activities leading up to the march on Rome and thus making it perfectly clear that the revolution had been purely political. The *squadristi* heroes of this revolution were canonized as the Old Guard (*Vecchia Guardia*), again emphasizing their place in the past rather than in the present. (Alessandro Blasetti's film *Vecchia Guardia,* released in 1934, was the best artistic effort to glorify squadrism as a historical phenomenon.) Anyone looking for evidence of Fascism as a "continuing revolution" did not find it in the 1932 exhibition or in any other feature of Italian public life. Squadrism and syndicalism were dead, the ethical state was an empty phrase, and corporatism was a façade for favoring the interests of the employers and the state over those of the workers.

But neither Mussolini, nor Starace (party secretary from 1931 to 1939), not the old and new ideologues were content with the bureaucratized "corporate state." Mussolini soon turned to imperialism. . . .

The government permitted the expression of all sorts of heterodox ideas as long as these ideas did not challenge the regime itself, but it ignored them completely in formulating its own policies, especially imperialism. Although the conquest of Ethiopia rallied the Italian people behind the regime as no other Fascist policy did, it was not a uniquely Fascist goal. Mussolini's war with Ethiopia was popular not because it transformed Italy into a new Roman Empire but because it united the Italians against the opposition of the League of Nations and especially against the English. The *Duce's* words and manner expressed the strong emotional need of millions of Italians to overcompensate for the patronizing and often contemptuous attitude of Anglo-Saxons, Frenchmen, and other Europeans toward them. The victory over Ethiopia seemed to fulfill this need until Mussolini spoiled the illusion that Italy could create its own "place in the sun" by making the country a junior partner of Germany.

The disastrous end of their regime—defeated and overthrown in a war it could easily have avoided—has overshadowed the domestic goals of the Fascists during their rise to power. From 1919–1925 the majority of the Black Shirts were alienated young men, a self-styled "lost generation," determined to overthrow the liberal establishment by violent means and restore a "sick society" to health. Mussolini had already gone through this phase before 1914; he simply used the revolutionary activism of the *squadristi* to make himself a dictator. He also exploited the demagogic nationalism made popular by D'Annunzio (the archexample of the danger of the poet in politics) and the revolutionary syndicalist dreams of some of his older associates. Indeed his own revolutionary background made him think of himself as a Left-wing extremist up until late 1920. When he finally saw that such a role would get him nowhere, he abandoned it for that of a strike-breaking, anti-Bolshevik patriot. Yet once in office he could hardly be called a lackey of the existing "power structure."

To see Fascism primarily as an instrument of reactionary landowners and big businessmen is a misinterpretation of basic significance. Balbo and Farinacci, Rossoni and Lanzillo, and even

Mussolini himself hated the existing political, social, and cultural orders, whose leaders looked down on them as low-class rabble-rousers and who were only interested in using them in order to quell those revolutionaries who wanted to destroy the economic order as well. During the early 1920's the Fascists used the reactionary landowners and big businessmen as much as they were used by them in suppressing the Red menace. Their goal was not *counter*revolution but *another* revolution. The liberal regime was their ultimate enemy; in their struggle to subvert and overthrow it, they made the reactionaries their main allies and the Reds their main rivals. Their revolution destroyed the existing political system. The Fascists did not alter the class structure, but they made it possible for many young men of humble origin to rise to positions of power hitherto closed to them, and they gave many urban workers the illusions, albeit short-lived, of solidarity and of integration into the national society. They had nothing to offer culturally except empty rhetoric and a strained austerity in their style of public behavior. But then neither cultural poverty nor ideological disunity prevents people from being revolutionaries.

7 FROM   *Federico Chabod*
The Corporate State in Action

*What was Italian Fascism's much-touted "corporative system,"
how did it work in practice, and how was it related to Mussolini's
foreign adventures? To these questions the late Professor Chabod
offered some judicious answers.*

What was this corporative system? From 1926 onwards Fascism began to concern itself with the question of collective labour relations. The term "corporative" appeared officially for the first

SOURCE. Federico Chabod, *A History of Italian Fascism* (London: Weidenfeld and Nicolson, 1963), pp. 71–81. Reprinted by permission of the publisher.

time in a decree of 1 July 1926. On 21 April 1927 the Labour Charter came into being. (Fascism went in for striking phrases like this, designed to appeal to the imagination; thus we shall find Mussolini speaking of the "battle of the lira," the "battle for wheat," and so on; for the time being, it was the "Labour Charter." This Charter consisted of thirty articles which were to provide the framework of the corporative State. They proclaimed: "Work . . . is a social duty. In virtue of this, and this alone, it is protected by the State. All production forms a single whole from the national point of view; its aims are unitary and comprise the wellbeing of individual citizens and the development of national power" (Art. 2). We note at once the bringing together of the two terms: "the wellbeing of individual citizens" and "the development of national power." Economic life must depend on the State; it is no longer to be left to liberal individualism or to be the result of purely individual efforts. And for what end? For the greatness and power of the nation. Mussolini was to repeat this again. He reiterated that the existence of the corporations, as directive organs of the nation's economic life, was indispensable. On 5 February 1934 the law on the corporations was proclaimed. On 10 November Mussolini spoke as follows to the twenty-two corporations which had just been set up: "What is the aim? At home, to establish an organization which will gradually and inflexibly reduce the distance between the greatest and the least or non-existent possibilities in life. This is what I call a higher 'social justice' . . . In relation to the outer world, the object of the corporation is to increase constantly the global power of the nation to further the ends of its expansion in the world." On the one hand social peace, on the other the nation's power and expansion (in other words, a national or rather nationalistic aim) —these two ideas are constantly associated alike in 1927 and in 1934.

At that time we were in the midst of the economic crisis, and Mussolini declared: "This is a crisis of the system as a whole, not a crisis within the system." When he said these words the crisis had already reached its peak: the worst year was, in fact, 1932, and he was speaking in 1934. But in 1934, if the crisis was getting no worse, it was still going on. Let us try to clarify the sentence: "The crisis in which we and the whole world are living is not a crisis within the system: it is a crisis of the system as a whole."

That meant that it was not a case of a crisis that could be cured, even by exceptional methods, so long as the principles of liberal economy were adhered to. On the contrary, it was a crisis of the system itself. It was therefore necessary to create a new economic system, disciplined and organized with a view to the collective benefit. The sphere of economy must henceforth fall within the world of the State. The time of *laissez-faire* was at an end.

From the point of view of the economic system, the following observations may be made. During the First World War an economic system had been created in Italy designed to meet war-time needs and largely controlled from above. The Government had to organize and direct the Commissions for the collection and distribution of supplies. Reasons of State imposed State control of the economy. Such control fostered the view that the State should provide against all difficulties: it was its job to look after everyone, from the workers and peasants to the big industrialists.

After the war, from 1919 onwards a reaction against this system set in. Everywhere people were saying: "Let us alone, we've had enough of restrictions. The State ought to stop interfering in our affairs . . ." (unless it was a question of an industry or a bank having to meet a deficit . . . in which case the State was sharply reminded of its "duty"). Fascism signified a return to control. But this time it meant not a temporary or limited return, dictated by military needs, but a definite and permanent economic policy. It meant autarky.

This, at any rate, was how Mussolini saw it. He created twenty-two corporations which together embraced all the different branches of the whole economy. The National Council of Corporations became the supreme arbiter of the country's economic life.

By 1939 Italy had advanced so far along this road that, as had already been foreshadowed in 1936, the corporations replaced the old system of political representation. A law of 19 January 1939 abolished the Chamber of Deputies; the new Chamber was called the Chamber of Fasces and Corporations, and it, together with the Senate which was still appointed by the King, was to collaborate with the Government in drawing up laws. It was all perfectly simple. There was no likelihood of the slightest opposition. The Chamber of Deputies no longer had the task of discussing the Government's policy; it merely had to "collaborate."

This meant a quite new electoral system; and the country was already on the threshold of war. The Chamber was to consist of the members of the Fascist Grand Council and the National Council of Corporations; consequently any member of the latter body automatically belonged also to the Chamber of Fasces. Thus, by the time the war began, even from a formal point of view the old organization of legislative power had completely vanished in Italy.

The corporative system nevertheless achieved for a time a reputation to be reckoned with. Between 1931 and 1935, that is to say up to the Abyssinian war, it was the centre of real interest. Many young people and university students believed they saw in it a way of circumventing and overcoming the absolute dictatorship. Groups consisting chiefly of such young people who chafed against the idea of a permanent personal dictatorship came to feel at a certain point that thanks to the evolution of the corporative system there might be a possibility of emerging from the grip of the dictatorship and advancing in a new direction. During this period the corporative system was the one topic that could be discussed in Italy with some degree of freedom. A congress on the subject held in Ferrara gave rise to a quite lively debate. The two themes stressed both in the corporative laws and in Mussolini's speeches, those of "social justice" and "expansion in the world," lent themselves to two different interpretations. Was the new system to be used as an instrument in the struggle for a nationalist policy, or was it really to be the means of producing a radical transformation in the structure of Italian society—to realize, in fact, that social justice that was so much talked about? Thus out of the discussions on the corporative system there soon emerged a definite leftward trend championing ideas of social reform. Fascists were to be found who proclaimed the necessity for a "war on capitalism." One result of this was to awaken fresh interest in Fascism, especially among young people. Might it not, they urged, after all contain possibilities of development which would enable them to overcome the purely dictatorial phase?

The corporative system also attracted attention abroad. Economists discussed its efficacy and significance, asking what it really meant: was it all just words, or was it something new which deserved to be studied and might open up new prospects in political and social organization?

The corporative system took shape and came to completion in a period in which life in Italy, as in other countries, was disturbed by an economic crisis. The great crisis of 1929 had immediate repercussions in Italy as in the rest of the world; between 1930 and 1934 the crisis of prices, salaries, and wages hit a poor country such as Italy very seriously. Prices collapsed. In agriculture, they had stood at 413.4 in 1930 and fell to 297.9 in 1934. Wheat prices, reckoned at 100 in 1928, fell to 79.7 in 1931 and 66.8 in 1934; but they rose again in 1935 and 1936, reaching 88.6 in the latter year. On the other hand wine, another important product in Italy's economy, remained in a state of crisis: on the basis of 1928 = 100, the price index in 1936 was 35.6. At the same time, wages were falling even more sharply: taking the same basis of 1928 = 100, by 1934 they were down to 71.8 (according, that is, to the official statistics, but the actual facts were even worse; between 1926 and 1934 agricultural workers could be reckoned to have lost the major part of their earnings). In 1933 there were 336,000 unemployed in agriculture alone.

The crisis also hit landowners, who were the more vulnerable because they were perennially burdened with debts to the banks. In the period before 1929, at a time of rising prices, many of them had borrowed in order to carry out improvements on their properties. Thus the crisis in prices and incomes was particularly serious for them.

In industry, the worst period of depression was around 1932. The available data on the subject are very vague. There are two sets of figures, those compiled by the Ministry of Corporations and those of the General Confederation of Industry. All we can do here is to point out the differences between them. The Confederation of Industry's figures for industrial production, taking 1929 = 100, are 72.4 in 1932, and 81 in 1935, at the beginning of the Abyssinian war. (The Ministry's figures, on the other hand, are 1928 = 100, 1932 = 73, 1935 = 102.4.) The textile industry, a basic feature of Italy's economic life, was the worst hit: while the average figure for industrial production in 1932 was 72.4, that for textiles was 67.4. Prices of manufactured goods fell from 440 in 1930 to 317.2 in 1934. In 1932, out of 2,939 industrial concerns with a capital of over a million lire, 1,216 showed a deficit. There was also a considerable decline in industrial wages between 1926 and 1934.

There were, of course, some good sides to the question. Wheat production undeniably increased: in the period 1931–5 it reached a yearly average of around 73 million quintals, with a maximum harvest, in the exceptionally good year of 1933, of 81 million quintals, representing an average yield of 16 quintals per hectare. Consumption needs were thus almost, if not quite (except in 1933), satisfied by national production. This meant a considerable reduction in Italy's purchases on foreign markets.

But despite all this, Italy's economy found itself involved in a very serious crisis: just how serious it was can be deduced from the increase in unemployment (officially reaching 961,000 unemployed in 1934, of whom 750,000, or 21 per cent of all workers, were in industry and trade) and from the statistics given above, even allowing for their variations.

The prevailing atmosphere of crisis no doubt accounts for the lively tone of the discussions of this period. What was to be done? Should the economy come completely under the control of the State, or not? And if not, what was the point of organizing it according to the corporative system? Did that system represent the future form of the State, which would eventually allow the phase of dictatorship to be surmounted, or was it only a propaganda move, a tactical weapon like so many others, created to delude public opinion? And, above all, of the two objectives proclaimed, social justice and national power, which was the true one, the real end in view?

So we come to the Abyssinian venture. That venture inaugurated a new period, the last period of Fascism. It signified a completely new turn in every respect in Mussolini's dictatorship. Up till then it must be admitted that Fascism, despite the economic crisis, seemed and indeed was soundly established. The years between 1929 and 1934 were the time when the régime achieved the greatest general support. I have briefly indicated the reasons for this support, differing widely in kind but all tending towards the same result.

There seemed to be no way out. The determined anti-Fascists were either in prison, or carrying on the struggle underground constantly harassed by the police, or condemned to restricting their activities to the cultural sphere. For the rest of the populace, the sole reaction was indifference or resignation.

THE ABYSSINIAN WAR AND ITS CONSEQUENCES
FOR THE RÉGIME

Reasons for Italy's Entry into the Abyssinian War. The Abyssinian war marked a profound change in the situation. The newspapers, in attempting to explain it, declared that it was a vital necessity for Italy, given her superabundant population. That problem undoubtedly existed: excess of population in relation to the country's productive capacity was a very real problem, then as now, and it was certainly not Fascism that created it. The rising birth-rate had by 1936 brought the population to nearly 43 million. Emigration to the United States and Latin America had been much reduced after the introduction of restrictions on entry by the United States in 1921. The pre-war average of 600,-000 emigrants a year fell to 70,000 in the years 1931–40. Large-scale public works of land reclamation were undertaken, such as the draining of the Pontine marshes, and this meant not only an increase of production but also a means of establishing a number of peasant families on the land. Indeed, in the plains near Rome the population rose in a few years from some hundreds to 60,000. But such measures were totally inadequate to meet the need for employment.

Nevertheless, this was not the main reason which led Mussolini to embark on the Abyssinian campaign; nor was it the need to divert attention from the serious economic situation, though that probably influenced him to a minor extent. But the political motive was the main one in Mussolini's mind—the motive of Italy's power and national prestige. I have already referred to Mussolini's indifference in 1919–22 to principles and programmes. But once he had achieved power and got what he wanted, as time went on he became increasingly sensitive to the doctrinaire influence of nationalism. Sometimes sudden flashes of recollection of his Socialist past would rise up in him, and then for a brief period he would talk about social justice. But his real concern now was nationalism. More and more his eyes turned to the outer world and his mind to Italy's power and prestige, which was bound up with his own personal power and prestige. This is the inevitable law of dictatorships: success abroad is made to compensate for the loss of liberty at home.

In September 1935 the decision was already taken. War broke

out on 3 October. I do not propose to consider the Abyssinian question from the international angle, for that would involve reconstructing the whole history of European politics and the relations between the Great Powers in 1935–6. What is important here are the internal repercussions of the war on the Fascist régime and the state of mind of the Italians. At first, when the Abyssinian question seemed to boil down to a simple matter of colonial expansion, the attitude of most people in Italy was one of indifference and even hostility. It was a great mistake on the part of the British to make popular a war which would otherwise have been anything but that. This result was brought about through the threat of the British fleet in the Mediterranean in September 1935—a threat which was in fact mere bluff, for the fleet was not in a state to risk an encounter. But the British move played into Mussolini's hands at home in bringing about a change in public opinion, which lost sight of Abyssinia and believed that Italy herself was actually threatened by Britain.

The proclamation of the Empire in May 1936 introduced changes of grave consequence. Those who had entertained hopes of the corporative State, of social peace and justice, now said: "Obviously, it was all just words and bluff. The real aim is clearly conquest . . . and a policy of that kind is all to the advantage of the industrialists." It was quite true that immediately after the outbreak of war the industrial situation suddenly improved. In 1931 the net profit of share companies in relation to invested capital was 0.08 per cent; in 1932, the peak year of the crisis, it was −1.38, rising in 1933 to 2.18 and in 1934 to 4.10 per cent. But it was in 1935–6 that profits began to increase really noticeably. In 1935 they rose to 5.74 and in 1936 to 7.28 per cent. This meant that industry, and in particular the war industries, was reaping immediate benefit from the war.

Nevertheless, it seems to me difficult to maintain that the war was decided on because of pressure from the industrialists. Obviously they derived advantages from it; but it is going too far to suggest that it was their hope of these gains that caused the war. Its origin, it must be stressed, was political.

In any case, if there had ever been any prospect of social reform, it had now vanished. The hopes centring round the corporative State were quickly dispersed, and all illusions crumbled.

Intervention in Spain and Alignment with Germany. Italy's intervention in the Spanish civil war followed hard on the heels of the Abyssinian war, and from 1935 onwards the country's industry was working for military ends. The rising power of the big industrial groups acted as a brake on any genuine attempt at establishing greater social justice. Autarky assumed an increasingly political and military character; and the corporative State came more and more to resemble a State preparing for war. Germany, which was beginning to exercise an influence on Fascism and especially on Mussolini, was there to provide an example. The aim was to create a great State able to burst its bonds abroad in the same way that the Fascist Party had in the past shown itself able to break up the structure of the old ruling classes.

Illusions about corporativism fell to the ground. The ideal of "social justice" gave way to that of "Italy's expansion and world power." Other illusions, too, were destined to disappear. . . .

In March 1938 came Hitler's occupation of Vienna and Austria. This time Mussolini did nothing. His speech in the Senate justifying Italy's passivity was perhaps the most disappointing he had ever made. You could sense the man's embarrassment at his inability to provide the Senate with an explanation of his conduct. Though he was a dictator to whom everything was permitted, he seemed profoundly disconcerted. This passive attitude on Mussolini's part provoked immediate and definite repercussions. The unquestionable prestige which he had enjoyed abroad crumbled, and the balance that had hitherto governed, at least formally, the relations between Italy and Germany was shattered: henceforward Fascism was dragged in the wage of Nazism.

PART TWO

German National Socialism

8 FROM Geoffrey Barraclough
The Rise of National Socialism

The unified, rapidly industrializing Germany that Bismarck had built with the help of the Prussian army preserved the enormous political power, huge landed estates, and social influence of the Junkers, from whose ranks the officers of the army itself were largely drawn. The rapid growth of large-scale capitalism in commerce and industry added big business to the German power structure and a self-conscious, but hardly revolutionary, working class to the forces working for political and economic democracy. World War I heightened the influence of the army and big business, and did nothing to undermine the position of the landed aristocracy. Paradoxically—and tragically—these power blocs, having lost the war, were spared the onus of defeat and the difficulties of reconstruction: with help from President Woodrow Wilson, they washed their hands of all the problems they had so largely engendered and suddenly told the Social Democrats, for whom they had very little use, that it was now up to them to govern Germany. The Social Democratic politicians, who had no previous experience of governmental authority and who were more anxious to "legitimize" their authority by careful adherence to constitutional forms than they were to make democracy workable by cutting its enemies down to size through substantial reforms, botched the job. This is the point at which the

SOURCE. Geoffrey Barraclough, *The Origins of Modern Germany*, 2nd edition, pp. 440–452. (Oxford: Basil Blackwell & Mott Ltd., 1947). Reprinted by permission of the publisher.

following selection from Professor Barraclough's history of Germany begins.

The hopes and expectations roused in 1918 by by the defeat of Hohenzollern militarism were doomed to disappointment; the opportunity to remodel German society and German political life in a new international framework was missed. Three main factors explain the failure. First, the army, the unswerving guardian of the old order, although defeated on the field of battle, remained in existence, a potent reactionary factor in German politics. Secondly, the German people was not left free to reshape German society on democratic lines; instead it was subjected to Allied pressure and, at many important points, to Allied veto, and the creation of an efficient government capable of expressing the will of the German people was subordinated to the national interests of the victorious Entente. Thirdly, the German leaders who emerged after the flight of William II on November 9th, 1918, proved totally incapable of rising to the magnitude of the tasks facing them; instead of placing themselves at the head of the revolutionary forces which the military failure had released, and carrying through a total reorganization of German society, they sought to steer a cautious middle course and let slip the opportunity for fundamental change which alone could have assured the prevalence of the strong democratic forces in Germany.

Nothing was clearer, after the experiences of the period 1871–1918, than the fact that without a real shift in economic and social power, transferring political initiative from the Junkers and capitalist interests to the people, the introduction of a lasting democratic régime was impossible. The revolution which began on November 3rd, 1918, with the naval mutiny at Kiel and spread rapidly through the whole country between November 6th and 9th, opened up the immediate prospect of fundamental change; for it was a spontaneous movement directed by workers' and soldiers' councils elected everywhere in workshops, mines, docks and barracks, and this movement, at its first congress in December 1918, formulated demands which included the socialization of key industries and, pending its replacement by a people's militia, a purge of the army. If put into effect, this programme would, without doubt, have brought about the fundamental shift in economic and political power which was the essential pre-condition for the success of the whole revolutionary movement. But it was not put into effect. Gröner, who had replaced Ludendorff on October 26th as quartermaster-general, informed the government that he and the entire High Command would resign immediately, if the workers' proposals were put into effect; and before this ultimatum the government, although it was a Social Democratic government nominated by the workers' and soldiers' councils, capitulated. Instead of proceeding to the immediate socialization of industry at the moment when the workers' councils were in effective control of the workshops, it set up a "Socialization Commission" with employers' and workers' representatives, which naturally failed to reach agreement and soon faded ineffectually out of existence. Instead of partitioning the great estates east of the Elbe, it appointed another commission to study the problem. Instead of convoking immediately a national assembly, it decided to hold elections on January 19th, 1919, and refused to take any decisive steps until the new assembly's authorization had been secured. Thus, through the anxious, cautious constitutionalism of the Social Democrat leaders, Ebert and Scheidemann, none of the three fundamental reforms—democratization of the army, public control of heavy industry, redistribution of landed property—was secured; and the reason was that to secure them it would have been necessary to rely on extra-parliamentary means and have recourse to popular pressure. Such a policy was alien to the whole character of the Social Democratic leadership, which had for decades past known no higher aim than the attainment of parliamentary democracy and the representation in parliament of working-class interests. No minister had the courage to accept the responsibility of using the power actually in his possession in order to change the internal balance of power or to secure control of its mainsprings. Hence the constituent assembly which met at Weimar to draft a new constitution in the spring of 1919 succeeded only in grafting mechanical devices, such as proportional representation, parliamentary sovereignty and the referendum, on to the existing body politic; but under this liberal cloak the old economic and political forces of the Hohenzollern Empire continued to exist undisturbed. The Weimar Constitution established the external forms of political liberty, but without the changes in social and economic power which alone could give them vitality.

This initial failure, from which recovery in fact proved impossible, was not, of course, the result of a deliberate betrayal of the revolution by the Social Democrat leaders. It was due to the limitations of the men themselves, and it was due in part at least to external circumstances, before which they capitulated. They were afraid lest economic experiment might produce chaos, and expose Germany to the famine and misery from which Russia was then suffering. They were afraid lest social change, easily denounced as "Bolshevism," might lead to Allied intervention. These fears were not unjustified. All the Entente powers were preoccupied with the dangers of "Bolshevism" and particularly afraid of "Bolshevik revolution" in Germany, and were prepared to co-operate with the German army to preserve "order" in Germany, just as they co-operated with it in the Baltic states and the Ukraine against the Russian revolution. Thus the German revolution was from the very beginning frustrated by the hostility of the victorious powers, and there is no reason to believe that they would have shrunk from the use of force and the terrible weapon of blockade, as occurred in the case of Hungary, had it proved necessary to oppose fundamental social change. In these circumstances a policy of radical social and economic reform undoubtedly entailed serious risks, and could not have been carried through without heavy sacrifices on the part of the German people, for which the rulers were unwilling to take responsibility. The failure of the Social Democrat leaders—and, indeed, of the Allied powers—was the failure to realize that these risks were no less serious than the dangers of doing nothing, which gave reaction the chance of recovery. Instead they concentrated their efforts, partly to keep Allied confidence, partly to prove their ability to govern, on the maintenance of law and order. Because they feared that their removal would have disturbed the smooth running of the public services, they left the officials of the old imperial bureaucracy in office; because they feared that his dismissal would complicate demobilization and worsen relations with the victorious Entente, they retained Hindenburg, and with him the core of the old army. Worse still, the preoccupation of the government with law and order brought it into conflict with the very forces whose spontaneous action had brought about the November revolution of 1918. This conflict came to a head in January 1919, when the Social Democrat defence minister, Gustav Noske, called in the notorious Free Corps to crush the left-wing labour movement in Berlin, and followed up this success by a series of punitive expeditions extending from Bremen to Munich. The civil war which raged for the first three months of 1919 sealed the fate of the German republic; the victory of Ebert and Noske was hailed as a victory for the middle-class republic and democracy over Bolshevism, but in reality it was a victory for the Free Corps, for the anti-democratic forces which had come to the rescue of the republic to prevent social change, but which only tolerated the republican government temporarily as the lesser evil. On the other hand, it created a breach between the right and left wings of the German labour movement so deep that it could never again be bridged, and this breach permanently crippled the powers of resistance of the democratic forces when reaction had sufficiently recovered to raise its head. The attitude of the people to the republican government was aptly described as early as June 1919, by one of the more foresighted Social Democrat ministers, Rudolf Wissel; "in spite of the Revolution," he said,

"the hopes of the people have been disappointed. The government has not lived up to the expectations of the people. We have, indeed, constructed a formal political democracy, but fundamentally we have done no more than continue the programme initiated by the imperial government of Prince Max of Baden. We drew up the constitution without real participation by the people. We failed to satisfy the masses, because we had no proper programme.

Essentially, we have governed in the old ways, and there has been little sign of a new spirit informing the old procedure. We have not been able to influence the course of the Revolution in such a way that Germany is swayed by a new inspiration. The esssential character of German civilization and social life is little altered, and that little not always for the better. The people believes that the achievements of the Revolution are of a merely negative character, that the only change is in the set of persons exercising military and bureaucratic authority, and that the present principles of government do not differ in essentials from those of the old régime . . . It is my belief that the verdict of history on the national assembly and on us, the members of the government, will be hard and bitter."

The attitude of profound disillusion with the Republic reflected in Wissel's speech of June 14th, 1919, was confirmed by the terms of the peace settlement, which was signed a few days later, on June 28th. It is no part of our business to enter into the unending controversy which, ever since 1919, has centred round the Treaty of Versailles, its relation to Wilson's Fourteen Points and to the fundamental principle of "self-determination" on which they were based. It is enough to note that certain facts impressed themselves on Germans of all parties. First, the settlement was "dictated," i.e. contrary to previous international practice the French representative, Clemenceau, prevented verbal negotiations. Secondly, in spite of Allied lip-service to the principles of "self-determination" wide areas were detached from Germany without plebiscite, the *Anschluss* of Germany and Austria was vetoed by France, and over three and a half million Germans, who actively sought incorporation in the new Austrian republic, were compelled against their will to remain in the new Czechoslovak state. Thirdly, despite the assurance of "a free, openminded and absolutely impartial adjustment of all colonial claims," Germany was deprived of all her colonies without a formal hearing. Fourthly, the German representatives were compelled—in contradiction to Wilson's promise of December 4th, 1917, that "no people shall be . . . punished because the responsible rulers of a single country have themselves done deep and abominable wrong"—to sign a statement that Germany, along with the other defeated powers, "accepted the responsibility" for causing all the loss and damage brought about by a war "imposed upon" the world "by the aggression of Germany and her allies." Fifthly, on the basis of this clause "reparations" amounting to 132 milliard gold marks were demanded, i.e. twenty-two times the amount demanded of Russia by the German imperial government in the notorious treaty of Brest-Litovsk. Juridically, it is possible to justify most, if not all, of these terms as part of a settlement imposed by a conqueror on a vanquished enemy; but they were a serious blow to the forces of German democracy which, confident in the promises of Wilson and Lloyd George, sincerely believed that Germany, once it had overthrown the

Hohenzollerns and broken, under a democratic régime, with the traditions of Hohenzollern imperialism, could count on terms such as would enable the republic to take its place in the comity of nations. Instead it was saddled with "guilt" for the policy of William II, in which it had no share and which it had rejected. The inexpediency of this policy, the moving spirit behind which was France, was recognized at the time by both Wilson and Lloyd George; but, with their hands tied by secret treaties concluded during the war, neither was able to put up a firm opposition to the policy of France, as enunciated by Clemenceau, and which once again, as so often in the past, was not easy to reconcile with lasting European settlement. French demands for the annexation of the Saar and the separation of the Rhineland from Germany were successfully resisted; but French policy created ineradicable suspicions and there were few Germans—or, for the matter of that, few Americans or Englishmen—who did not believe that the principle of national "self-determination," as applied in the case of Poland and Czechoslovakia, had been used as a cloak for a French attempt to raise clients in the east, whose political function was to aid France in perpetuating Germany's defeat. Such a view was unjust to Wilson and Lloyd George; but it reflected the policy of Poincaré and Clemenceau. The pursuit of unrepentant power-politics at a moment when, in Europe and America, a new generation, reacting against pre-war imperialism, was prepared to renounce power-politics as an instrument of national interests, destroyed the hopes of 1919. In Germany the effects of this policy were disastrous. The treatment of the new German republic as a weak and defeated power equated the republic and weakness and thereby strengthened immeasurably the hand of all reactionary forces within Germany opposed to the republican régime. "The outcome," as a leading English historian has said, "has been the Germany of Hitler that we know."

To follow in detail the well-known story of the years from 1919 to 1933, from Versailles to Hitler, is not necessary, for in all essentials, due to the folly of the Allies and the failures of the German democratic leaders, the die was, as early as 1919, already cast. From the start, the Weimar republic failed to arouse the enthusiasm or anchor the loyalties of the great majority of Germans. On the right, the nationalist sections, which still exerted immense pressure, regarded it as a transitory stage on the road towards the reassertion both of their old preponderance at home and of German military power in Europe. On the left, the bulk of the German people regarded it as an equally transitory stage towards a form of political organization which really reflected popular aspirations. What backing it had came from the middle classes; but owing to the unbalanced development of German society from the time of the Thirty Years War onwards, the middle classes were too weak and politically too unreliable to carry alone the burden of government, and if they had to choose between the left, with the threat of real social change, and the reactionary groups of the right, they preferred co-operation with the latter. This weakness played into the hands of the right wing sections, which soon established themselves in a position of control, enabling them to use the constitutional machinery of government for their own ends. It played into the hands of the Reichswehr which, in 1923, forced the working-class governments of Saxony and Thuringia to resign. Still more ominous, it played into the hands of the industrialists, who after November 1922, loosed the horrors of inflation on Germany in order, while freeing themselves from internal indebtedness, to destroy the resources of organized labour. With the appointment of Wilhelm Cuno, director-general of the Hamburg-Amerika line, as prime minister in 1923, the undisguised rule of large-scale capital began; the attack on the Eight Hour Day and the refusal to meet expenditure by direct taxation revealed that the notorious Hugo Stinnes and Fritz Thyssen were in the saddle. Heavy industry prospered as never before, while the nation was starving and the state facing bankruptcy; from 1920 to 1924 the power of capital increased immensely, and its hold was consolidated after 1924 in the course of reconstruction and rationalization and the progress of industrial monopoly.

These tendencies were concealed but in no way reversed by the period of relative prosperity between 1924 and 1929. The fact that business, supported by foreign loans, was again back to normal brought a gradual slackening of tension, particularly in the industrial field, and it seemed as though democracy were at last functioning properly and booking results in the form of improved housing conditions and similar social benefits. But the effect of such social services, however welcome in themselves, on German economic structure was nil, and under the surface the old balance of power persisted. The election of Hindenburg to the presidency in 1925 was an index of the true situation; it revealed in a flash how far removed from power the democratic and progressive forces were in the mid-twenties. Although "the great majority of Germans" wanted to "settle down to a life of peace and international co-operation," the power of heavy industry, which ultimately could only keep going on the basis of a great armaments programme, continued to expand. The desire of the German people for a continuation of peace and democratic government was expressed in the elections of 1928, when the Social Democratic vote, which had slumped in 1921 and 1923, rose to over nine millions, and the two working-class parties, the Social Democrats and the Communists, together secured over 42 per cent of the seats in the Reichstag. But this swing in the voting, unaccompanied by any move to break the economic and social power of the industrial and landed classes, did not imply a fundamental strengthening of democratic government. It only needed a break in prosperity to bring back into the open the antagonism between the army and the great industrial monopolies on the one hand, and the people on the other. This came in 1929. Already by February 1929, the total number of unemployed had passed the three million mark. In October 1929, there followed the Wall Street crash. Short-term loans—fifty per cent of the loans to Germany totalling twenty milliard marks were short-term, unconsolidated loans—were recalled; German industry, dependent on foreign markets because low wages and drastic inequalities of income prevented the creation of a great domestic market, slumped rapidly; and unemployment increased apace. By January 1933, official unemployment figures passed the six million mark, but the actual number of unemployed rose to between eight and nine millions.

The crisis which set in during 1929 brought about the death of the German republic. Having failed to enlist the support of the working-classes, the republic was dependent upon the middle-class vote of the centre parties. But the middle classes, the small property owners and shopkeepers, who had already been hit by the inflation, collapsed before the slump of 1929–1933; the rapid decline in the workers' purchasing power ruined millions of small shopkeepers, tradesmen, artisans, black-coated workers and peasants, and these elements—which had, as a class, nothing to hope from a working-class movement—turned to Hitler and the specious promises of National Socialism. The National Socialist vote, which had rallied only 800,000 supporters in 1923, rose in September 1930, to almost 6,500,000, and the National Socialists emerged from insignificance to the position of second strongest party in the Reichstag. Two years later, in July 1932, the vote for Hitler more than doubled, rising to 13,700,000 out of a total electorate of some 45,000,000—the highest vote ever obtained by National Socialism in a free election. This success, born of the crisis, was secured at the expense of the middle and upper class parties; as indicated in the table overleaf, the working-class electorate—in spite of the miseries of poverty and unemployment—tenaciously resisted the blandishments of Hitler's demagogy, and the working-class vote, cast in favour of Social Democracy and Communism, stood firm throughout, just as the Catholic vote stood firm. The split in the left-wing forces, and in particular the purblind policy of the Communist leaders, unhappily facilitated the rise of National Socialism; but the real strength of Hitlerism lay in the support of the privileged classes, of the industrial "kings," the Junkers and the army, with the connivance of parallel interests in England and France. At no stage from the onset of the crisis in 1929 until 1933 had Hitler any hope of succeeding to power, even by unconstitutional means, without the backing of capitalist and reactionary interests. Before the inauguration of the Hitler terror National Socialism never obtained the support of more than one-third of the German people; and in the last six months of 1932 National Socialist strength actually decreased by 2,000,000 votes. When on January 30th, 1933, Hitler was made chancellor,

VOTES (IN MILLIONS) AT GENERAL ELECTIONS, 1924–1932

Parties	1924	1928	1930	July 1932	Nov. 1932
Working-class parties (Social Democrats and Communists)	10.5	12.3	13.0	13.1	13.1
Middle-class parties (excluding Centre party)	13.2	12.9	10.3	4.0	5.3
Catholic Centre Party	4.1	3.7	4.1	4.5	4.2
National Socialists	0.9	0.8	6.4	13.7	11.7

it was not through the support of, but rather as the result of a conspiracy against the German people; his rise to power was the work of Hindenburg representing the army, of Papen representing the aristocracy, of Hugenberg, the press-lord, and of Thyssen representing the industrialists of the Ruhr. It was this unholy alliance which led the German people to ruin and Europe to war.

The alliance with National Socialism, contrived by Hugenberg as early as 1929 and formally concluded by Papen at the beginning of 1933, was only the last step in a campaign against the democratic republic and the German people waged by the "national" interests ever since the onset of the economic crisis in 1929. For these interests the depression was a welcome opportunity—"this," one industrialist declared, "is the crisis we need!" —to break for ever the power of the German people to guide their own destinies, and in particular to destroy organized labour. As in the inflation they had attacked the Eight Hour Day, so in 1930 they immediately launched an attack on the unemployment fund, while resisting the Social Democratic attempt to impose direct taxes. The resignation of the Social Democrat ministers and the appointment of Brüning as chancellor in March 1930, marked their success, and the end of democratic government in Germany. Thenceforward government was in the hands of a narrow clique, which, supported by the army and the executive under Hindenburg, dispensed with constitutional forms and ruled by emergency decrees. These decrees were directed ruthlessly against the working classes: indirect taxation was increased, new capitation taxes were introduced, bearing as heavily on the poor as on the rich, food prices were forced up in the interests of the agriculturists by heavy import duties. At the same time a devastating policy of deflation was introduced to support German export industries, and huge sums were paid out as subsidies to the bankrupt Junker agriculturists east of the Elbe. It was class rule on a huge scale, unashamedly pursuing class interests at the expense of the people; its naked use of force was seen when on July 20th, 1932, Papen ousted the constitutional labour government of Prussia and entrusted executive power to General von Rundstedt. But it was class rule on a narrow foundation. The working class parties, as has been seen, remained firm, holding the allegiance of their traditional supporters to the last; but the "nationalist" parties underwent a disastrous decline. The scandals of the *Osthilfe*, the endless government subsidies to its Junker supporters, could not be hushed up; the demand for a redistribution of the land in eastern Germany for the benefit of the people could not be quelled. On the other hand, there were limits, even in Germany in 1933, to an unconcealed dictatorship based on the armed forces. For landowners and industrialists alike the sharp decline in the National Socialist vote in November 1932, and the signs of a swing to the extreme left, were ominous trends, alarming indications that the day of reckoning was at hand. Their alliance with Hitler was the sequel. It was an alliance reluctantly entered into; but, their own supporters having disintegrated, it was necessary as a device to throw a cloak of popular support over the dictatorship which, under a rotting veil, they had exercised ever since the Social Democrats were forced out of office in March 1930.

The calculations of the "national" industrial and Junker interests miscarried. When on January 30th, 1933, Hindenburg and Papen called in Hitler, hoping thereby to stabilize their own hold over Germany, they gave themselves and Germany a new master, implacable and ruthless.

9 FROM
The First Program of the Nazi Party
February 24, 1920

Like the first program of the Italian Fascist movement, the first program (1920) of the National Socialist German Workers' Party [NSDAP]—as it called itself—contained anticapitalist demands. But, in contrast to the Fascist program, the Nazi program was also virulently nationalistic and anti-Semitic. Nothing came of the anticapitalism; but a good deal came of the nationalism and the racism.

SOURCE. Michael Oakeshott, *The Social and Political Doctrines of Contemporary Europe* (New York: Cambridge University Press, 1942), pp. 190–193. Reprinted by permission of the publisher.

The programme of the German Workers' Party is limited as to period. The leaders have no intention, once the aims announced in it have been achieved, of setting up fresh ones, so as to ensure the continued existence of the Party by the artificially increased discontent of the masses.

1. We demand, on the basis of the right of national self-determination, the union of all Germans to form one Great Germany.

2. We demand juridical equality for the German people in its dealings with other nations, and the abolition of the Peace Treaties of Versailles and St Germain.

3. We demand territory and soil (colonies) for the nourishment of our people and for settling our surplus population.

4. None but members of the nation may be citizens of the State. None but those of German blood, whatever their creed, may be members of the nation. No Jew, therefore, may be considered a member of the nation.

5. Anyone who is not a citizen of the State may live in Germany only as a guest and must be regarded as subject to the laws governing aliens.

6. The right to determine the leadership and laws of the State is to be enjoyed by the citizens of the State alone. We demand, therefore, that all official appointments of whatever kind, whether in the Reich, in the one or other of the federal states, or in the municipalities, shall be held by citizens of the State alone.

We oppose the corrupt Parliamentary custom of filling public offices merely with a view to party considerations, and without reference to character or capacity.

7. We demand that the State shall make it one of its chief duties to provide work and the means of livelihood for the citizens of the State. If it is not possible to provide for the entire population living within the confines of the State, foreign nationals (non-citizens of the State) must be excluded (expatriated).

8. All further non-German immigration must be prevented. We demand that all non-Germans who have entered Germany subsequently to 2 August 1914 shall be required forthwith to depart from the Reich.

9. All citizens of the State shall be equal as regards rights and duties.

10. It must be the first duty of every citizen of the State to

work with his mind or with his body. The activities of the individual must not clash with the interests of the whole, but must be pursued within the framework of the national activity and must be for the general good.

11. We demand, therefore, the abolition of incomes unearned by work, and emancipation from the slavery of interest charges.

12. Because of the enormous sacrifice of life and property demanded of a nation by every war, personal profit through war must be regarded as a crime against the nation. We demand, therefore, the complete confiscation of all war profits.

13. We demand the nationalization of all business combines (trusts).

14. We demand that the great industries shall be organized on a profit-sharing basis.

15. We demand an extensive development of provision for old age.

16. We demand the creation and maintenance of a healthy middle class; the immediate communalization of the big department stores and the lease of the various departments at a low rate to small traders, and that the greatest consideration shall be shown to all small traders supplying goods to the State, the federal states or the municipalities.

17. We demand a programme of land reform suitable to our national requirements, the enactment of a law for confiscation without compensation of land for communal purposes, the abolition of ground rents, and the prohibition of all speculation in land.

18. We demand a ruthless campaign against all whose activities are injurious to the common interest. Oppressors of the nation, usurers, profiteers, etc., must be punished with death, whatever their creed or race.

19. We demand that the Roman Code, which serves the materialistic world order, shall be replaced by a system of German Common Law.

20. The State must undertake a thorough reconstruction of our national system of education, with the aim of giving to every capable and industrious German the benefits of a higher education and therewith the capacity to take his place in the leadership of the nation. The curricula of all educational establishments must be brought into line with the necessities of practical life.

With the first dawn of intelligence, the schools must aim at teaching the pupil to know what the State stands for (instruction in citizenship). We demand educational facilities for specially gifted children of poor parents, whatever their class or occupation, at the expense of the State.

21. The State must concern itself with raising the standard of health in the nation by exercising its guardianship over mothers and infants, by prohibiting child labour, and by increasing bodily efficiency by legally obligatory gymnastics and sports, and by the extensive support of clubs engaged in the physical training of the young.

22. We demand the abolition of a paid army and the foundation of a national army.

23. We demand legal measures against intentional political lies and their dissemination in the Press. In order to facilitate the creation of a German national Press, we demand:

(a) that all editors of newspapers and all contributors, employing the German language, shall be members of the nation;

(b) that special permission from the State shall be necessary before non-German newspapers may appear. These must not be printed in the German language;

(c) that non-Germans shall be prohibited by law from participation financially in, or from influencing German newspapers, and that the penalty for contravention of this law shall be suppression of any such newspaper and the immediate deportation of the non-German concerned in it.

It must be forbidden to publish newspapers which do not conduce to the national welfare. We demand the legal prosecution of all tendencies in art and literature of a kind calculated to disintegrate our national life, and the suppression of institutions which militate against the above-mentioned requirements.

24. We demand liberty for all religious denominations in the State, in so far as they are not a danger to it and do not militate against the moral sense of the German race.

The Party, as such, stands for a positive Christianity, but does not bind itself in the matter of creed to any particular confession. It is strenuously opposed to the Jewish-materialist spirit within and without the Party, and is convinced that our nation can only achieve permanent well-being from within on the principle of placing the common interests before self-interest.

25. That all the foregoing demands may be realized, we demand the creation of a strong central power of of the Reich; the unconditional authority of the central Parliament over the entire Reich and its organization; the formation of Diets and vocational Chambers for the purpose of administering in the various federal States the general laws promulgated by the Reich.

The leaders of the Party swear to proceed regardless of consequences—if necessary to sacrifice their lives—in securing the fulfilment of the foregoing points.

Munich, 24 February 1920

10 FROM *Adolf Hitler*
On Idealism and on Winning the Masses Over
(from Mein Kampf*)*

The first volume of Hitler's Mein Kampf, *from which the following passages are taken, was written in 1923–1924, while its author, thanks to the pro-Nazi sympathies of the judicial authorities, served only one year of a five-year sentence for participating in an attempted coup d'etat. It contains, inter alia, a substantial amount of what Nazis and Nazi-sympathizers counted as a theory, philosophy, or world-view* [Weltanschauung]. *After the collapse of the Third Reich many Germans—eminent historians among them—were fond of claiming that they (together with most Germans) had not known in time what Hitler stood for, since few people read his long and tedious two volume opus (nearly 800 pages in the standard edition). But since most of what Hitler stood for could also be gleaned from press and radio, from Nazi speeches, posters, leaflets and tactics, the alibi is not very impressive.*

The curious definition of idealism in the first passage requires no comment. But it may be worth pointing to the remarkable contents of the second passage: the leader of a movement which claimed to represent the true interests of the German people thought that the people could be won over to its cause only by

SOURCE. Adolf Hitler, *Mein Kampf.*

such purely demagogic tactics as those that he was frank enough to outline.

IDEALISM

It is not intellectual talent which accounts for the Aryan's ability to be culturally creative and constructive. Such talent by itself would only enable him always to act destructively, never to organize; for in essence all organization ultimately depends on the individual's renouncing his claims to his own views and interests and sacrificing both for the good of the group. . . .

This disposition to set self-interest aside so that the community may be preserved is in fact the prime requisite for all truly human culture. It alone makes possible the great achievements of mankind, which afford scant reward to the man who undertakes them but bring untold blessings to posterity. Indeed, it is only in terms of this disposition that it becomes comprehensible that so many people should bear a penurious existence in dignity, should put up with a life which affords them nothing but poverty and frugality while it provides the greater whole with the basis of existence. Every workman, every peasant, every inventor, civil servant, etc., who labors [*schafft*] without ever being able to achieve happiness or prosperity for himself is a bearer of this lofty idea, even if he remains wholly unaware of the deeper significance of his conduct.

But if this is true of labor, which sustains mankind and is the basis of all human progress, it is true in even greater measure of the defense of man and his culture. To lay down one's own life for the community is the highest expression of the spirit of sacrifice. Only in this way can what human hands have built be kept from being torn down by other human hands or destroyed by nature.

[It is no accident that] our German language has a word which in a magnificent way denotes conduct based on this spirit: doing one's duty [*Pflichterfüllung*]—which means serving the community instead of contenting oneself.

We have a word for the basic disposition which underlies conduct of this kind in contrast to egoism and selfishness—idealism.

By 'idealism' we mean only the ability of the individual to sacrifice himself for the whole, for his fellow-men.

THE MASSES MUST BE WON OVER

Since, then, a favorable solution of Germany's future depends on the great mass of our people being won over for the nation, winning them over must be the highest and mightiest task of a movement which is not to spend itself in achieving short-run gains, a movement which must instead gauge its every action and inaction wholly in terms of presumable long-range consequences.

Thus in the year 1919 we were already clear that, as its foremost goal, the new movement must carry out the nationalization of the masses. This led to a number of considerations which, from a tactical point of view, seemed imperative:

(1) To win the masses for the [movement of] national resurgence, no social sacrifice is too great.

Whatever economic concessions are made today to the nation's working people, they are as nothing compared with how much the whole nation stands to gain if these concessions contribute to restoring the broad masses to their nation. Only short-sighted narrow-mindedness of a kind unfortunately quite common among our entrepreneurs can fail to see that there can be no lasting economic recovery for them—and therefore no future economic gains—if the inner social solidarity of our nation is not restored. . . .

(2) The broad masses can be educated to the national cause only by the round-about way of an upswing in social conditions, since this alone can create the general economic conditions which enable the individual to partake of the nation's cultural goods.

(3) The "nationalization" of the broad masses can never be accomplished by means of half-measures, by harping feebly on a so-called objective view of the situation. [It can be accomplished] only by taking a ruthless and fanatically one-sided attitude towards the goal for which one is striving. . . .

The broad masses of a people consist neither of professors nor of diplomats. The meagre abstract knowledge they dispose of prompts them to take their cues from the realm of emotion [rather than from that of reflection]. That is where their disposition is rooted, be it positive or negative. They are receptive only to wholehearted affirmation or wholehearted negation, never to a halfway position that wavers between them. But at the same time it is this emotional orientation which makes them so extraordinarily stable. Faith is harder to shake than knowledge, love is less changeable than respect, hatred is more enduring than aversion. The impetus to the mightiest upheavals on this earth has always consisted less in any objective knowledge by which the masses have been dominated than in the fanaticism with which they have been inspired and sometimes in the hysteria which has driven them on.

Anyone who wants to win the broad masses [for his cause] must know the key that will open their heart. It is not labelled "objectivity," i.e. weakness, but "will and power."

(4) One can succeed in winning the soul of the people only if, together with the positive campaign one carries on in behalf of one's objectives, one also destroys him who opposes these objectives.

At all times the people sees ruthless attack on an adversary as proof that it is in the right. To refrain from destroying an enemy is to make the people uncertain that they are in the right; they may even take it as a sign that they are in the wrong.

The broad masses are only a piece of nature. The mutual handshake of people who claim to differ is incomprehensible to them. What they want is the victory of the stronger and the destruction of the weak or his absolute subjugation.

It will be possible to nationalize our masses only if, while the positive struggle for the soul of our people is carried on, the international [forces] which are poisoning them are exterminated.

11 FROM   *Walther Hofer*
The Nazi Program and Its Adherents

For purposes of analysis, Hitler's accession to dictatorial power in Germany may be divided into three phases: (1) his rise to political prominence as leader of a mass movement that in 1932 was, though still a minority party, the largest single party in the Reichstag; (2) the intrigues among reactionary members of the Junker-industrialist establishment that saw in the Nazi movement a source of popular support for their own policies, and gave Hitler high but unlimited authority by offering him the Chancellorship in a coalition cabinet composed of National Socialists and Nationalists; (3) the so-called "legal," "national" "revolution"—the actual establishment of dictatorial power—that Hitler and company carried through after his installation as Chancellor. The first of these is dealt with by Hofer (below) the second is touched on by Barraclough (above); the third is analyzed in Bracher's article (below), to which the present editor has added a note.

[Nazi ideology comprised racism, antisemitism, the idea of the Leader,˙ the quest for *Lebensraum*, and the notion that life is combat.] Hitler himself once summarized his outlook as follows, "It is combat that has made man great . . . . Everything man has achieved he owes to his creativity and his brutality. . . . The whole of life can be summed up in three propositions: combat is the father of all things, virtue is a matter of race [Blut], leadership is primary and decisive." . . .

On the basis of this ideology the Nazis then quite consistently fought against everything that was incompatible with this new political religion: against democracy and parliamentary government, against liberalism and humanism, against pacifism and the League of Nations, against Bolshevism and capitalism, and above

SOURCE. Walther Hofer, *Die Diktatur Hitlers bis zum Beginn des zweiten Weltkriegs* (Vol. 4/II, Handbuch der Deutschen Geschichte, Athenaion 1960) pp. 13–15. Reprinted by permission of the publisher.

all and constantly against that universal scapegoat, the Jew. The national-socialist myth was anti-rationalistic and anti-humanistic, anti-democratic and anti-liberal. It was also anti-historical in its desire to defy tradition and establish a radically new order.

It was precisely this catalog of negations which enabled the NSDAP to become a mass movement, which made it possible for the party, from 1929 on, to gather to itself the rapidly growing mass of the discontented, however difficult it might be to square their dissimilar expectations with one another. The followers of National Socialism *were at one above all in a negative sense*, in what they rejected. What was principally at work here was the psychological role played by widespread political and social resentment, and above all a rampant nationalism which completely stifled political common sense and equated patriotism [die Idee des Nationalen] with disloyalty to the Republic and with the rejection of democracy. As to what was to take the place of the old regime, as to what the "new Order" of that supposed heaven-on-earth, the "Third Reich," was actually to look like—as to these matters the Nazi leaders either said nothing at all or gave out promises couched in terms so vague as to appeal to all and sundry. They were very fond of evading the concrete and practical issues of politics, society and economy by means of such demagogic slogans as: There's got to be a complete change, or, as Gregor Strasser once put it, *"National Socialism is the opposite of what we have today."* What made it all the more difficult for Nazis to give answers to concrete questions was the fact that throughout the whole period there were violent quarrels within the party as to where it should stand—for instance, on the relation of nationalism to socialism.

It would therefore be a great mistake to suppose that all those who gave the Nazis their vote fully accepted Nazi ideology, or that they so much as knew what it was. Enormous numbers of people read their own notions and wishes into National Socialism, or adhered to those parts of the motley party program that spoke to their own feelings and desires, without worrying too much about how *those* particular promises squared with others. What drew masses of people into Hitler's movement was dissatisfaction with things as they were—politically, socially, and economically—and the expectation that their desires would be fulfilled by those dynamic National Socialists. In this way Hitler's party became a mass movement not only of the uprooted, the impoverished, the dissatisfied, and the desperate, but also of idealists, opportunists, adventurists and careerists. There were the nationalists who longed for a great and strong Reich; the ex-officers who dreamed of a new Army or even of fresh glory on the battle-field; the peasants who hoped to be rid of their debts and to get better prices for their produce; there were the industrialists who saw in Hitler a partner in their fight against the unions and who doubtless also expected to make a pretty penny out of rearmament; there were the countless petty bourgeois who put the blame for the loss of their savings or their business on the existing government or on the Jews; there were also the unemployed who turned away from the Marxist parties in disappointment and joined Hitler's Storm Troopers; finally, there were the intellectuals, who were greatly impressed by the Nazi movement's demand for total power and who looked forward to being relieved of the risks and responsibilities of thinking for themselves by the Nazi ideology's claim to absolute validity.

The very vagueness of its program made it possible for National Socialism to appear to be at once anti-capitalist and anti-proletarian, to be aiming simultaneously at restoration and revolution, to be both nationalistic and socialistic. As a result, the party was able to garner support among all social strata. It is accordingly difficult to make a sociological analysis of the party structure. But it can at least be shown that the party appealed most to the lower middle class which had been affected economically and financially by the Great Depression, and had no firm political convictions. This class felt itself to be threatened by capitalism as much as by communism and wanted to guard itself against being pushed into the lowest strata of society. It was the very stratum to which Hitler himself belonged. He knew their feelings and their resentments and consciously aimed his propaganda at them. A comparison of the social structure of the NSDAP with that of the German population as a whole shows that in 1930 workers made up forty-five percent of the total population, but only twenty-eight percent of the NSDAP, whereas the percentage of white-collar workers and self-employed in the party's ranks was twice as great as in the nation at large. Civil servants and peasants, too, constituted a larger proportion of the party membership than they did of the country. The dynamic and all too often ruthless and brutal conduct of the Nazis also made a great impression on the politically naive and socially largely uprooted young people, who are always, as the psychologists tell us, prone to romantic and adventuristic radicalism. There was a Nazi party slogan that said "National Socialism is the will of the young—organized." Youthful support made itself apparent in party membership: whereas in the NSDAP thirty-eight percent of the members were under thirty, in the SPD only nineteen percent belonged to that age group.

Though it was thus clearly a mass movement which led to Hitler's rise, the movement itself did not actually bring him to power, for all that his Storm Troopers contributed to the terrorizing of the public and the politicians. *Hitler did not achieve the objective he had set himself*: to win a majority in the Weimar Republic. In the end he became Chancellor thanks to the collusion [Zusammenspiel] of a number of elements which to a great extent operated outside the realm of political accountability: first and foremost the . . . clique around President von Hindenburg, a number of economic interest groups, and the leaders of the army. Hitler owed the "seizure of power" to one of the many extra-parliamentary *intrigues* which were characteristic of the political atmosphere of the dying Republic in its final months.

12 FROM   *Karl Dietrich Bracher*
           The National Socialist Seizure of Power

The key to understanding the character and course of events in Germany from 1933 to 1934 is the slogan "legal revolution." From the beginning, the National Socialist leaders emphasized

SOURCE. From *The Path to Dictatorship 1918–1933, Ten Essays by German Scholars* by Karl Dietrich Bracher, pp. 115–128. Copyright © 1966 by Doubleday & Company, Inc., and reprinted by permission. *The Road to Dictatorship 1918–1933*, pp. 113–125. Reprinted by permission of Oswald Wolff Publishers Ltd., London.

that Hitler's takeover of the government, although it marked the beginning of a revolution with profound and far-reaching effects, was an entirely legal, constitutional proceeding. The paradox of *legal revolution* forcibly joined two mutually contradictory political axioms. But the tactic of claiming legality for revolutionary aims was more than a propaganda trick. As a step-by-step examination of the course of events shows, it determined the decisive phases and circumstances that made this new-type seizure of power so seductive, and all legal, political, and intellectual opposition so difficult, indeed—in the opinion of many—practically impossible.

This also applies to the preliminary events. The lasting significance of the abortive *Putsch* of 1923 is that it made Hitler realize that a direct assault on the existing order was doomed to failure. Even in such a crisis year as 1923 the forces of status quo in the government and Army had not let themselves be taken unawares. Despite the Republic's internal and external difficulties, the democratic parties and the trade unions had a capacity to retaliate that the *Putsch* could not overcome. Above all, the very belief in authority among the middle classes and the civil service that made life so difficult for the Weimar Republic was at the same time a significant obstacle to any attempted coup. Although these same circles gave strong support to the Republic's critics and opponents, it had already become evident that this adherence to legality, order, and security—although not to freedom—was one of the basic traditions of the German state. This was the reason why the revolution of 1918 did not run its full course, the Kapp *Putsch* of 1920 failed, and the year 1923 was surmounted, despite all dictatorial appetites, including the Army's and Seeckt's.

The path was thereby marked out for the NSDAP, which had re-formed in 1924–1925 after Hitler's imprisonment, and although his position seemed weak and without a future measured by the rules of parliamentary democracy, Hitler followed it consistently in the face of impatient revolutionaries in the party and the SA. The German people's aversion to open revolution—which was deeply rooted after the experiences of 1848 and 1918—showed the tactician of legal revolution a new possibility, which he ultimately used: a dictatorship supported by the German President. A double weakness in the Weimar Constitution made this possible.

First, most legal experts agree that the Weimar Constitution (unlike the Basic Law of 1949) did not prevent constitutional means from being used to undermine and eventually to destroy its very substance. This is precisely what happened after 1930, especially in 1932, and the process was completed in 1933 with the Reichstag Fire Ordinance and the Enabling Act. Hitler himself clearly described the possibility of destroying the Constitution legally in his famous "oath of legality" at the Leipzig Reichswehr trial in 1930, when he declared with impunity before the court:

"The Constitution prescribes only the arena of the struggle; it does not specify the goal. We shall enter the legitimate organizations and in this way make our party the decisive factor. Once we possess the constitutional rights to do so, we shall, of course, cast the state in the mold that we consider to be the right one."

Goebbels had made a still clearer and more cynical declaration as far back as 1928 in his newspaper *Der Angriff* (The Attack):

"We are entering the Reichstag to supply ourselves, in that arsenal of democracy, with democracy's own weapons. We become Reichstag deputies in order to paralyze the spirit of Weimar with its own aid. If democracy is so stupid as to pay our transportation and daily expenses for these 'services' of ours, that is its own affair. . . . We come as enemies! As the wolf breaks into the sheepfold, so we come. . . ."

At this point the NSDAP was still far from having a decisive role in the Reichstag, and even at the time of its greatest expansion, in the summer of 1932, it did not have much more than one-third of the parliamentary seats. The legal path to dictatorship by way of becoming a majority party remained blocked for Hitler, especially as the November 1932 elections showed a distinct decline in the number of National Socialist supporters and sympathizers.

But a second weakness in the Weimar system offered a way out of the seemingly insoluble dilemma posed by the policy of legality. This was the possibility of a Presidentially appointed government without the support of parliament and even in opposition to it. The essential point in the almost endless discussion of this subject seems to me to be the fact that the dictatorial powers of the Presidency under the famous, or infamous, Article 48 of the Weimar Constitution, which was originally designed to safeguard the democratic order against postwar attempts to overthrow it, under a differently disposed President had the exactly opposite effect. Even the Bruening cabinet in 1930, and certainly the authoritarian Papen and Schleicher cabinets in 1932, made it clear that the legal possibility of an extra-parliamentary or actually anti-parliamentary government would inevitably paralyze the Reichstag and the parties. The ever-present resort to emergency powers gave these cabinets a convenient escape from political responsibility and at the same time accustomed the public to the authoritarian concepts of government that journalists and even political scientists were propagating more and more intensely.

The outbreak of the world economic crisis with its catastrophic consequences and the legendary fame of the Reich President who was connected with these authoritarian concepts quickly turned the possibilities of authoritarian infiltration into reality. Of the mass of political and personal factors that led to Hitler's chancellorships, only one need be considered here: in the give and take of negotiations, Hitler's basic demand remained unchanged—he, too, as Chancellor, must have the emergency powers of Article 48. Stressing "legality," Hitler made his way into the government, not as the leader of a working parliamentary majority coalition (as misleading apologists still suggest) but through the authoritarian gap in the Weimar Constitution, and immediately set about destroying the Constitution he had just taken an oath to defend. That formally correct oath he regarded as the symbol and end of his successful policy of legality. Now the actual seizure of power began. Now the tactics of legality had to be combined with the strategy of revolution to form the specific technique of seizing power that in a short time was to outplay, eliminate, or regiment all safeguards and counter-forces, political, social and intellectual. To accomplish this, a second magic phrase was needed to sow confusion, turn aside opponents, and deceive allies. This phrase was the official slogan, the "national revolution."

This was the catchphrase during the decisive development of the *legal revolution* in the first seven weeks of Hitler's Presidential government, which ended with the Enabling Act of March 23–24, 1933. Ever since the campaign against the Young Plan in the fall of 1929, and, more important, since the Harzburg Front two years later, Hitler's tactic had been to find support among industry, the Army, and the big agrarian interests in a *national opposition* of right-wing parties. But Hitler would no longer be merely a drum-beater and spearhead of the movement, to be dropped later by his conservative nationalist partners: 1923 had taught him a lesson. His alliance with the reactionary right was now only a means to gain strength for the battle against the Republic. Under stress the alliance invariably fell apart, as it did in the Presidential elections of 1932 when Hitler ran against Hindenburg and the Stahlhelm candidate Duesterberg. But in Germany's straitened circumstances at the turn of the year 1932–1933 Hitler readily seized on Papen's offer to renew the alliance, because now the conservative partners—Papen, Hugenberg, the German National party, the Stahlhelm and its backers in industry—were prepared to subordinate themselves to a government under National Socialist leadership. The result was a last-minute revival of the Harzburg Front at a moment of crisis in the Nazi party when there was a general economic recovery and the Schleicher government began making determined counter-plans. This disguising of the National Socialist bid for power as a nonpartisan *national revolution* offered a superb ideological facade for carrying out the *legal revolution* constitutionally—which became evident when the new government was formed. There were only three National Socialists as against eight conservatives in the cabinet; the conservatives held the Vice Chancellorship and such important ministries as Defense, Economics, and Foreign Affairs, and furthermore felt confident of the support of President Hindenburg and the Army. The outward appearance was of a coalition cabinet in which National Socialist ambitions could easily be checked. Papen, thinking of his own secure ties to Hindenburg, exulted at having "engaged" Hitler. To another conservative who criticized his moves, Papen declared: "What more do you want? I have Hindenburg's trust. In less than two months we will have pushed Hitler so far into the corner that he'll be squeaking." As it turned out, it was not the Nazis but their partners, the self-confident "pushers," who were themselves pushed. Even before the new "government of national concentration" took the oath of office on January 30th, Hitler's superior strength as Reich Chancellor had become obvious. Unlike his coalition partners, Hitler knew what he wanted. By the time he succeeded in dissolving the Reichstag for a second time over Hugenberg's opposition, the non-Nazi front within the cabinet had been shattered. This was demonstrated again and again from one cabinet meeting to the next. As a matter of fact, resistance on the cabinet level never materialized, although it was not until considerably later that the Nazis occupied most of the cabinet posts.

This was not solely the result of the illusions and opportunism with which the German-Nationalist partners had entered the coalition, confidently relying on their prestige and influence in economic, social, and military circles. It was also because, contrary to all appearances, there was a thoroughly unequal division of power in the government and in politics generally. The positions of Chancellor, Reich Minister of Interior (Frick), and Prussian Minister of Interior (Goering) were all the Nazis needed to carry out the *legal revolution* virtually without their cabinet colleagues and to convert the *national revolution* into a National Socialist seizure of power. This was facilitated by the fact that the new Defense Minister, Blomberg, proved particularly susceptible to Nazi wiles and promises of rearmament. Deceived by Hitler's protestation of nationalism and Christianity, Hindenburg allowed himself to be misused, and during February 1933 a series of emergency decrees were issued under the fateful Article 48 which created the base from which the National Socialists were able to control public life and direct or suppress almost at will.

There was, to be sure, some breach of legality. The decree of February 6, 1933 that gave Goering practically full control over Prussia openly disregarded the Supreme Court verdict in the Prussia dispute of 1932. Rigid restrictions were placed on freedom of the press and of assembly. Above all, the Reichstag fire was made the pretext for a suspension of basic rights that lasted for the entire twelve years of the Third Reich. All these things far exceeded the limits of the Constitution. Yet a seeming legality was preserved since the authorities charged with the protection of the Constitution—the Reich President, the Army, the cabinet ministers, political parties, trade unions, and the courts—made no resistance or effective protest against these acts of violence. This was precisely the purpose that the façade of the "national revolution" was meant to serve during these first weeks. Hitler's nationalist partners, despite massive experience to the contrary, clung to this fiction until they were maneuvered out of all power —practically, by the end of March, ultimately and finally, by June 1933. They clung all the more readily—and soon anxiously

—because they hoped to avert thereby the threat of the National Socialists ruling alone. Instead they made it possible for Hitler to achieve this, legally and without risk. Allies like Hugenberg realized this when it was too late; accomplices like Papen do not realize it even today.

Thus the ruse of *legal revolution* achieved full effect only through the second ruse of *national revolution*, which reached its peak in March 1933. Despite propaganda and terror, the Reichstag elections of March 5th unexpectedly failed to confirm Hitler's claim to sole power; they gave a majority not to the National Socialist party alone, but to the *national concentration* of Nazis and German Nationalists. Hitler therefore once again made an emphatic appeal to the nationalists to preserve the alliance. In observing the "Day of Potsdam" on March 21st, he repeated the professions of conservative nationalism that had marked the new government's first days, the declarations that had made such a lasting impression on the middle classes, the civil service, and the Army, and had diverted their attention from the terrorist acts of Nazi functionaries that accompanied the NSDAP's seizure of power. Hugenberg now soothed his supporters by quoting the German proverb, "When you are planing lumber, shavings have to fly." They had to be convinced that the work in which "the shavings were flying" was the construction of their kind of Germany—nationalist-authoritarian in their sense, and preferably monarchist; so the new propaganda virtuoso, Goebbels, staged a symbolic rite over the coffin of Frederick the Great in the Garrison Church of Potsdam in the presence of Hindenburg and the Crown Prince.

In the same spirit the state's black, red, and gold flag had been previously transformed into the black, white, and red flag of the *national revolution*. Thus Hitler's black, white, and red partners could hardly oppose this new breach of the Constitution when, once again, the pretense was maintained that National Socialist ambitions were being subordinated to the common goal; after all, the swastika flag had been made only *one* of the banners of the *national revolution*.

Two days later the reality of the National Socialist seizure of power stood fully revealed with the passage of the Enabling Act. So strong was the national appeal and so heavy the pressure of accomplished facts that the other middle-class parties—from the liberals to the center—felt obliged to agree to it. This Act of March 23, 1933, whereby the Reichstag yielded full legislative power to the government against the only remaining opposition —the left-wing parties—was in essence simply the end result of the permanent state of emergency that had been instituted by the fateful Ordinance of February 28th, after the Reichstag fire. It should also be stressed that Hitler violated many of the Act's restrictive provisions on which the middle-class parties had thought they could rely. This was true even of the passage of the Act by the Reichsrat, which was certainly not properly constituted once its constituent *Laender* had been "co-ordinated" by the coup d'état. Unquestionably one reason the middle-class parties agreed to the Enabling Act was because they believed this would induce the regime to stop issuing radical ordinances and to act within the constitutional legislative framework. But this, of course, was the fatal mirage created by the slogan *legal revolution*, which made the consolidation and completion of National Socialist rule so much swifter and more total than that of Italian Fascism.

In this, far more than in its concrete provisions, lay the tremendous significance of the Enabling Act. The Nazis' concrete acts of coercion and terrorism, including the brutal sentencing of the men involved in the July 20, 1944 plot, were based on the radical ordinances of the initial period, which provided a reassuring proof of the willing co-operation of the civil service and the courts, on which National Socialism, because it lacked trained personnel, was heavily dependent. As these ordinances had apparently come into being with all formal correctness, there could be no objection even to such a stormy and violent regime, although many of its "excesses" were regrettable "exceptions." Many high officials, as one can learn from the archives, comforted themselves with the fact that the revolution—which was inevitable in any case—proceeded with such neat and tidy legality. And thus they assured the *legal revolution* of all procedural success.

We can now see from the files of the ministries that this attitude quite palpably determined the advance work that was done on the Enabling Act by non-National Socialist officials of the Ministry of Interior. It can be observed in all the important work of legislation and administration, and is especially and fatally evident in the drafting of the basic Civil Service Law of April 7, 1933.

Euphemistically entitled "For the Restoration of the Career Civil Service," this law was designed to rid the service of not only Jewish officials but all political undesirables, and it opened the door to the dirty motives of careerism, personal enmities, and profitable informing on others. The same attitudes spreading from the civil service to all areas of social and cultural life, including the schools and universities, greatly facilitated the National Socialist seizure of power, binding citizens from the most varied walks of life to the regime with the ties of fear and advantage, breaking the backbone of their resistance, and thus establishing the most important prerequisites for a totalitarian system.

Deception and self-deception also help to account for the speed —which surprised even the Nazis themselves—with which the left was completely overpowered. By their flight from the government in 1930 and their capitulation without a struggle to Papen's coup in Prussia, the Social Democrats had largely excluded themselves from political responsibility even before 1933. And the Communists had taken every opportunity to stoke the fires of civil war and weaken democracy's defense. Contrary to the present assertions of East German Communist historians, it is an incontrovertible fact that the KPD made no effort to cooperate with the Socialists against the Nazis, but, on the contrary, continually stressed that the main struggle must be against the "social fascists," as they called the SPD. Thus the Communist leaders, for all their anti-fascist propaganda, helped to hasten the fall of the Prussian government, often making common cause with the National Socialists against the Republic—as they did in votes of nonconfidence, in the Prussian plebiscite of 1931, and in the Berlin transport strike of November 1932. Behind this grotesque yet significant collaboration lay the KPD's calculation that the fall of the Republic would make Germany ripe for the Communist revolution. Moscow, too, which had approved this course of action, obviously did not reckon on a long duration of the Nazi dictatorship but ascribed to it only a preparatory function. This explains Stalin's immediate efforts to remain on good terms with the Hitler regime and even to continue the collaboration between the Reichswehr and the Red Army. To gain these objectives, he accepted without real protest the persecution of German Communists. In fact, one of the first international acts of the Hitler regime—and also one of the first recognitions of it by a foreign power—was the renewal, at the end of April 1933, of the Russo-German Trade Agreement that had expired in 1931.

This tactic was a grandiose misreading on the Communists' part of the character of the National Socialist seizure of power. By denying it was a real revolution and explaining it simply as a crisis marking the end of monopoly capitalism, they helped to paralyze, fragment, and misdirect the opposition, especially the SPD, which in March 1933 still had a large following (20 per cent of the electorate) and a strong organization. Whereas Hitler first believed in the danger of a general strike, the SPD and trade-union leaders held fast to their faith in legality and considered it their primary task not to expose their organization to a ban, but to keep it intact until the moment when, after a few weeks, the Nazi regime would have played itself out. Contrary to the expectations of friend and foe, the SPD confined itself to the role of a legal opposition. In so doing, it became another victim of the tactic of legality. Its fallacious estimate of the stiuation was reinforced immediately after January 30, 1933 when it made its primary battle-cry opposition to the capitalist reactionaries, that is, the Hugenberg group, apparently regarding Hitler's partners as more dangerous than Hitler himself. Thus in its own way, which stemmed from Marxist ideas, the SPD, too, fell prey to the deceptive slogan of the *national revolution*. By the time a real opposition began to organize, it was too late.

Adroit manipulation of the *legal* and the *national revolutions* alone would probably not have been enough to make the transition from a constitutional state to a totalitarian dictatorship so smooth. Still another instrument, of which Hitler made skillful use, was necessary: the *dualism* of "state" and "party," which persisted even in the one-party state. Contrary to a widely accepted chiché, totalitarian rule by no means signifies a closed, monolithic, one-track organization. Nor is it true that totalitarian rule functions more rationally and efficiently and, by virtue of its leadership principle, is superior to the complicated pluralism of democracy. Hitler in fact never attempted to fuse party and state. In all areas of public life competing authorities continued to exist or were even newly created. Thus instead of the promised reform of the national government, the federal state was transformed into a maze of satrapies in which as many as three different authorities claimed primacy: *Reichsstatthalter* (Reich governor), the *Gau-*

leiter, and the Prime Minister. Instead of simplifying the machinery of government, the inflation of the leadership principle made the question of who was competent to do what still more complicated. The result was friction, wasted motion, duplication, and reduplication, which, it quickly became apparent, was not a sickness of the regime's infancy but a part of its very nature.

In fact, it is clear that this technique of ruling was largely conscious and had an important function, especially during the period of the seizure of power. By assuring trained personnel that the previous order would continue, it helped to win them over, and by allowing the individual official to believe he still had his own importance in the new system, it dimmed his realization that the duplication of functions granted him only a relative freedom, which could be withdrawn at any time, and that in decisive questions the Fuehrer and his apparatus of coercion and terror always had the last word. In this way, behind the façade of unchanged legal and judicial forms, beyond the reach of any court, the practice of "protective custody," the secret police, and the concentration camps developed.

This indicates the second function this dual, often multiple parallelism performed, even during the initial phases of the seizure. Only the Fuehrer stood above the confusion of authorities and echelons of command that left almost everyone his hopes and bound almost everyone, non-Nazi as well as Nazi, to the regime. The Fuehrer was the supreme judge whose omnipotence was ever more clearly underlined by the rivalries of subordinates and conflicts between state and party, Wehrmacht and Storm Troopers, industry and government. By playing the one off against the other and seeming to support each, he was able to assert and increase his own power all the more undisputedly. Hitler was a virtuoso of the art of *divide et impera.* Whether this was wholly intentional or merely an expression of the volatile moods of both the Fuehrer and his movement—which were closer to chaos than order—cannot be discussed here. But the effect of this controlled disorder cannot be denied when one remembers how grotesquely its contemporaries misinterpreted the National Socialist revolution.

These, in my opinion, are some of the most important elements that led to the fact that the National Socialist seizure of power, by means of the pseudo-legal national revolution, was followed by rapid success in many spheres besides the political. Indeed the "seizure" of even remote areas of public life and the speedy capitulation, often without resistance, of famous and renowned figures in business and trade associations, the churches, art, and science are part of the phenomena of the Nazi takeover. Its suggestive effect, which cannot be overestimated, played an important part, first in bringing about the rapid dissolution and elimination of political parties and private organizations, then in winning the assent of the population as a whole and rendering the opposition powerless.

EDITOR'S ADDENDUM

It is clear that, to carry through a "legal revolution" one must maintain a semblance of legality. To acquire dictatorial powers in a parliamentary democracy—which Germany was until March, 1933—one must be given such powers by vote of the legislature. Such a vote required a two thirds majority. To remain within the bounds of legality, Hitler would either have to win such a majority in the Reichstag, or be granted dictatorial powers by a combination of votes of his own and other parties.

To be sure, Hitler was prepared (as he frankly told a gathering of big business leaders on February 20, 1933), if he did not receive a majority in the forthcoming national elections on 5 March, to destroy the Left and to entrench the Nazis in power by other means. (The gentlemen in his audience received this message with evident satisfaction; they there and then pledged several million Reichsmark to Hitler's campaign funds; and through Gustav Krupp as their spokesman thanked the Führer for the clear presentation of his ideas, and expressed their wholehearted agreement.)

The Nazis did not receive even a bare majority in the elections of March 5. Despite the intimidation-and-propaganda campaign they had waged, they gained a small majority only in coalition with the Nationalist Party, the party of more traditionalist right-wing nationalism and conservatism. It was the continued support of these Nationalists, led by the millionaire press lord Alfred

Hugenberg, that now enabled Hitler to maintain the front of legality.

But the crucial step towards dictatorship was taken on March 23. An extraordinary session of the Reichstag, meeting in the Kroll Opera House, was to vote on a measure giving the cabinet dictatorial powers for five years. The 81 duly elected Communist representatives who would certainly have opposed it were excluded from the session. The 94 Social Democratic representatives voted to a man against the measure. But all the other parties, including the Catholic Center Party, which alone was large enough to have been able, in concert with the SPD, to vote the measure down, voted in favor.

The point of this addendum to Professor Bracher's fine analysis of the techniques adopted by the Nazis is a simple one: as long as Hitler adhered to the tactic of legality—or pseudolegality —it was still possible to oppose him by legal means. It may be true that, as Bracher says, the SPD, too, fell for the trick of the "legal" road to total power and failed to see that in fact a "revolution" was being carried out. But it is certainly the case that, had other parties voted with the SPD against the granting of dictatorial powers, Hitler would have been obliged either to forego dictatorial powers or openly to show his hand. The veil of legality would have been torn from him, the fraud of a "legal revolution" exposed for what it was, and millions of the German people (and the outside world) deprived of that chance for gross self-deception that, combined with the support and collusion of reactionary interests, made Hitler's path to dictatorship so smooth.

13 FROM   *Adolf Hitler*
The Solution to Germany's Problems

Hitler lost no time in cementing his relationship with the armed forces. On 3 February, three days after his appointment as Chancellor, he gave their leaders a sketch of his plans—military, economic and political. In a two and one-half hour talk, the gist of which is contained in the following notes, Hitler flatly contradicted the comparatively peaceful noises he had made in the official declaration of his government's intentions on 30 January. Then he had spoken of his sincere desire for peace with other countries and a policy of "reconciliation" within Germany; now he spoke of rearmament and conquest abroad, and of the "extermination of Marxism" and the suppression of all opposition at home. It is not recorded that the General Staff raised any objections. (Incidentally, the document reveals how Hitler understood the word "socialist.")

HITLER'S FIRST ADDRESS TO THE GENERALS

Berlin, 3 February 1933. Reichschancellor Hitler's remarks to the commanding officers of the army and the navy on the occasion of a visit to the house of General of the Infantry Freiherr von Hammerstein-Equord. Sole aim of overall policy: to regain political power. The whole administration of the state must be geared to this objective (all departments!).

1. Internal. Complete reversal of present domestic situation in Germany. No effectuation of any point of view opposed to this aim to be tolerated (pacifism!). Whoever won't let himself be persuaded must be made to submit. Extermination of Marxism root and branch. Youth and the whole people to adopt the view that only fighting can save us and that this idea must take

SOURCE. Walther Hofer, *Der Nationalsozialismus; Dokumente 1933–1945*, pp. 180–181. Copyright 1957 Fischer Bucherei KG, Frankfurt am Main. Reprinted by permission of S. Fischer Verlag.

precedence over everything else. (This already a reality: the millions [of members] of the Nazi movement. It will grow.) Every means to be used to make youth fit and to strengthen the will to fight. Death penalty for treason. Most rigorously authoritarian governance. Removal of the cancer of democracy!

2. External. Fight against Versailles. Equal rights in Geneva; but pointless if people not ready to fight. Concern about allies.

3. Economy! The peasant must be rescued! Policy of colonization! Future increase in exports pointless. World market [*Aufnahmefähigkeit der Welt*] is limited and there is overproduction everywhere. Colonization the only chance, part of army of unemployed to be put back in harness. But will take time and radical change not to be expected because *Lebensraum* [territory] too small for German people.

4. Build-up of Army most important prerequisite for achievement of objective; reconquest of political power. Universal military service must be reintroduced. But first government must make sure that those liable for military service are not poisoned by pacifism, Marxism, Bolshevism, etc. before they even do their military service or after they have done it.

How is political power to be used once it has been won? Can't say yet. Perhaps to fight for new foreign markets, perphaps— and no doubt preferably—conquest of new *Lebensraum* in the East and its ruthless Germanization. Certain that only political power and struggle can alter present economic conditions. All that can happen now—colonization—stop-gap measures. Army is most important and most socialist institution of the state. It is to remain non-political and non-partisan. Internal struggle not its affair, but Nazi organizations. In contrast to Italy, no intent of merging army and storm-troopers [i.e., party militia].—Most dangerous period is while Army is being built up. That will show whether France has statesmen; if it does, it won't give us time but will assault us (presumably together with its eastern satellites).

14 FROM *Dr. Ley, Nazi Labor Leader* *Address to the German Workers, May 2, 1933*

On May Day (1 May 1933)—the traditional Day of Labor and of the Left—Hitler held a Day of National Celebration and organized a huge rally of workers in Berlin. The next day, Storm Troopers, SS and Police attacked the workers' organizations, the unions: union officials were beaten, arrested, sent to concentration camps; union headquarters were smashed, pillaged, burnt; and union funds were "confiscated." While all this was going on, Dr. Robert Ley, head of the Nazi Labor Front, addressed the workers of Germany. An excerpt from his address follows.

What the unions of every political stripe, Red or Black, Christian or Independent, did not even begin to achieve; what remained a mere shadow even in the heyday of Marxism—a pathetic, pitiful, pale copy compared with the tremendous greatness of yesterday's events—these things National Socialism achieves at the first attempt.

[National Socialism] puts workman and peasant, artisan and white-collar worker—in a word, all productive Germans—into the very center of its thinking and doing and thus into the very center of its polity. Who was really the lackey of capitalism, who was the reactionary who tried to oppress you and rob you of your rights? Was it those red gangsters who for decades abused you—the kindly, honest, decent German worker—in order to deprive you and thereby the whole people of your rights and your inheritance? Or we, who at the cost of unimaginable sacrifice and suffering fought against the insanities and perversities of the Jews and their cronies? Three months of National Socialist rule are enough to prove to you: Adolf Hitler is your friend! Adolf

SOURCE. Walther Hofer, Ed., *Der Nationalsozialismus; Dokumente 1933–1945*, p. 60. Copyright 1957 Fischer Bücherei KG, Frankfurt am Main. Reprinted by permission of S. Fischer Verlag.

Hitler fights for your freedom! Adolf Hitler gives you sustenance [Brot]!

Today we are entering the second phase of the National Socialist Revolution. You may say: what do you want now? you already have absolute power. To be sure, we have power, but we do not yet have the whole people, we do not yet have you, the worker, one hundred percent, and it is precisely you we want; we won't leave you be until out of sincere conviction you unreservedly take your stand with us. You must be completely freed from the remaining fetters of Marxism in order that you may find your way back to your people.

For one thing we know: without the German worker there is no German people! Above all, we must make it impossible for your enemies, the Marxists and their fellow travellers, to betray you ever again.

15 FROM   *T. W. Mason*
Politics and Economics in Nazi Germany

The actual relationship between politics and economics in Nazi Germany has long been misunderstood. On the older Marxist view Nazism, like other fascisms, was simply the handmaiden of industrial and financial capitalism. On the cold war view of Nazism as "totalitarianism of the right" (paralleling Communist "totalitarianism of the left"), Nazism controlled economic enterprise almost as completely as did Communism. On the recently fashionable interpretation of fascism as a movement for modernization, the economic order of fascism is supposed to have aimed at the country's "development." That none of these views is satisfactory is made clear by Mr. Mason's article on the primacy of political considerations in the Nazi economy. Here is the concluding summary of his article.

SOURCE. From *The Nature of Fascism*, edited by S.J. Woolf, pp. 189–195. Copyright © 1968 by The Graduate School of Contemporary European Studies, University of Reading. Reprinted by permission of Random House, Inc.

From 1936 onwards the framework of economic action in Germany was increasingly defined by the political leadership. The needs of the economy were determined by political decisions, principally by decisions in foreign policy, and the satisfaction of these needs was provided for by military victories. The fact that numerous industrialists not only passively co-operated in the "Aryanization" of the economy, in the confiscation of firms in occupied territory, in the enslavement of many million people from eastern Europe and in the employment of concentration camp prisoners, but indeed often took the initiative in these actions, constitutes a damning judgment on the economic system whose essential organizing principle (competition) gave rise to such conduct. But it cannot be maintained that even these actions had an important formative influence on the history of the "Third Reich"; they rather filled out in a barbaric manner a framework which was already given. The large firms identified themselves with National Socialism for the sake of their own further economic development. Their desire for profit and expansion, which was fully met by the political system, together with the stubborn nationalism and their leaders did, however, bind them to a government on whose aims, inasmuch as they were subject to control at all, they had virtually no influence.

Only between 1934 and 1936 was there a degree of elastic cooperation between the economy and the state to the advantage of the economic system, and that only in a simulated form, for it was not based on a stable balance between the various class interests but on the terroristic suppression of the workers' organizations and on totalitarian propaganda. The political leadership constructed for itself a position of supremacy which in institutional terms was autonomous and unshakable and which, through its control of foreign policy, determined the direction of the system as a whole.

The seizure of power by the National Socialists can be traced back to a fundamental disintegration of bourgeois society in Germany, and the "primacy of politics" in its mature form was based on a renewed disintegration in the years 1936–8. This lack of unity and of co-ordination was by no means limited to the economy; on the contrary, it became the basic organizing principle of the National Socialist system of rule. A new stable and general representation of the people could not be achieved only by terror, propaganda and successes in foreign policy (i.e. through politics). This would have required a rational restructuring of society and neither in industry nor in the NSDAP was there the slightest inclination to attempt this. The old conflicts between agriculture and industry, capital and the working classes continued with the old intensity, though in new institutional forms. To these, new structural conflicts were added: *Gauleiter* against the central government, the party against the *Wehrmacht* and the civil service, the SS and the SD against everybody else. In 1938 General Keitel characterized the social and economic system as "a war of all against all." It was no less warlike for being fought in silence. Debates in Germany as elsewhere about the social distribution of the national wealth had always been public and ideological. The monolithic front which National Socialism wished to present to the outside world forbade such debate, and the ideology did not furnish a language in which it could be conducted. The differences between the various ruling groups were thus fought out behind closed doors and in the form of straightforward, unideological battles for power and economic resources. The constantly invoked "national community" of the propaganda concealed a reality in which the only acknowledged conformism was the cynical prosecution of one's own material interests; there developed as a result a broad, complex and "modern" pluralism of political and economic interests which, until the military recovery of the Soviet Union in 1942, defeated most of the government's efforts to simplify and unify the power structure. Until 1942 the system was held together by two things: the frenetic, aimless dynamism of expansion, in which the constant setting of new tasks compelled the various organizations and interests to co-operate with each other—standstill would have meant decay; and secondly, by the function of the *Fuehrerprinzip*. Hitler's alleged technique of extending his own sphere of influence by tactics of *divide et impera* was in reality a necessity dictated by the system, since the plurality of interests and organizations was already in existence.[1] Attempts to secure unitary structures of command foundered not so much on Hitler's desire to play the arbiter

[1] For the war period, there is evidence that Hitler *deliberately* created agencies with overlapping competences.

wherever he could, but on the power of those interest groups whose influence would have had to be curtailed if the various decisions on matters of principle were made. To decide between the rival claims of the Labour Front and industry, the contradictory interests of the farmers and the consumers or the different views of Goering and the *Gauleiter* on the need for stringent war economy measures was a very delicate and thankless task, which Hitler usually preferred simply to avoid. Speer was one of the few who could force him to take such decisions. Loyalty to the *Fuehrer* and the willingness of the leaders of state and party organs to accept Hitler's decisions often seemed to be the barrier standing between the 'Thousand Year Reich' and anarchy.

The self-destructive measures of the National Socialist system can only be understood in the context of the primacy of politics and of the material plurality of the power structure from which the state derived its autonomy. Among the first Polish Jews who were gassed in the extermination camps were thousands of skilled metal workers from Polish armament factories. This was in the autumn of 1942, at the turning point in the campaign against the Soviet Union, which was to increase still further the demands made by the *Wehrmacht* on the German war economy. The army emphasized the irrational nature of this action in view of the great shortage of skilled labour, but was unable to save the Jewish armament workers for industry. The general who made the formal complaint was relieved of his post. The same internal power relationship lay behind the use of scarce railway installations for the deportation of persecuted Jews towards the end of the war, instead of for the provisioning of the forces on the Eastern Front. The SS was able, by virtue of its monopoly over the information services and the machinery of terror, of its position outside the legal framework and lastly by virtue of Himmler's special relationship with Hitler, to execute its ideologically determined task of the destruction of the Jews to the material detriment of the whole system. The way in which the political sphere emancipated itself from all references to the needs of society is nowhere clearer than in the example of the SS, where the translation of ideology into practice was in flat contradiction to the interests of the war economy and yet was allowed to continue.

Another slightly less crass example was the decision of March

1942 to enslave the populations of eastern Europe systematically and put them at the disposal of the German war economy. Gauleiter Sauckel, who was given control over all labour deployment at that time, suggested that the problem of labour shortage could be solved by rationalization of the methods of production and by conscripting German women to work in industry. Slave labour, he maintained, was politically and technically unreliable, unproductive, and represented a "racial danger" to the German people. His programme was rejected by Hitler on the grounds that there was no time to rationalize the economy and that the German woman's place was in the home. After this a further five million "foreign and Russian workers" were brought forcibly into Germany, and Sauckel's doubts were confirmed. Again an ideologically determined policy triumphed over economic calculation.

Any attempt to find a common denominator in this ideology, to interpret it as if it were systematic, is doomed to failure. Goebbels and his team tended to understand and use the ideology as an instrument of domination, the contents of which could be manipulated almost at will. But in the end, the racial-ethical Utopia at its core was taken so seriously by the political leadership, in particular by Hitler and by the SS, that in decisive questions even the urgent material needs of the system were sacrificed to it. Precisely in the case of the destruction of the Jews and in the question of conscripting women into industry, the ideology was *not* any longer a necessary pillar of the system—as it perhaps had been in the early years of the Third Reich. For the destruction of the Jews was carried out *in secret* in Poland; and according to the reports of the security services on public opinion within Germany, the majority of the population would have approved of measures to compel women to work. What held the system together as late as 1944 was neither common interest nor a consensus, but fear—fear of "the Russian hordes," and of the now indiscriminate terror of the Gestapo.

Under the conditions of capitalist production, there is always something irrational about the assertion of a primacy of politics, since that which alone can legitimate this primacy, a commonweal, can only be simulated. It is only possible to talk of a rational primacy of politics when the state can act as trustee of a homogeneous society and base its policies on the needs and resources of the society. The radical nature of the primacy of politics under National Socialism, however, was rooted in the specific historical disintegration of bourgeois German society (1929–33), of German capitalism (1936–8), and of international politics in the 1930s. The immense political scope of the National Socialist government was not based on the confidence of a politically and economically homogeneous society; on the contrary, it was a result precisely of the disintegration of society. The coincidence of this with the collapse of the international order in the 1930s enabled the National Socialist state to achieve a degree of independence of society which is unparalleled in history. The development of the National Socialist system of rule tended inevitably towards *self-destruction,* for a political system which is not based on the requirements of social reproduction is no longer in a position to set itself limited and rational aims. This autonomy of the political sphere led to a blind, goal-less activism in all spheres of public life—a tendency to which the capitalist economy, based as it was on competition and the maximization of profit was particularly susceptible. The separation of the economic principle of competition from all institutional limitations designed to ensure the continued reproduction of society was part of the dialectic of National Socialism. The economic power of the state as an unlimited source of demand for armaments gave free rein to destructive tendencies in the economic system.

The fundamental irrationality of the system had in part its origin and found its concrete expression in the specific irrationality of the National Socialist ideology. This ideology was the product of a declining social class and came increasingly into conflict with the social realities created by National Socialist rule itself: the movement whose ideology had been directed towards the construction of a society of small traders, craftsmen, and smallholders brought about a tremendous acceleration in the process of concentration in industry and trade, and intensified the drift of population from the countryside into the towns; industry was concentrated in central and western Germany and drew increasingly on the population of the poorer eastern regions as a source of labour, thus making nonsense of the policy of colonizing and settling eastern Europe with German farmers —the one attempt at this in western Poland was a signal failure. Likewise the attempt to educate the working classes to idealism—

the workers had to be bought at a cost to military strength, and yet even this method did not suffice. In the end the ideology could only find a secure place in the "reality" of everyday life in and through the SS—and that only through terror and bureaucratic norms.

Fighting spirit and the willingness to make sacrifices on the one hand, and comprehensive military-economic planning on the other were only realized under pressure of imminent defeat. Self-destruction was the pre-ordained end of a system in which politics was synonymous with the boundless pursuit of political power; destruction its only achievement.

16 FROM *Helmut Krausnick*
The Attack on the Jewish Enemy

Anti-semitism was very nearly the only part of the Nazi movement's original program to be fully carried into practice after the Nazis' accession to power. The systematic persecution of the Jews began with the boycott of 1 April 1933 against Jewish businesses and Jews in the professions. It became part of the law of the land with the notorious Nuremberg Laws of November, 1935 which declared, inter alia, *that no Jew could be a citizen of the German state. The mixture of irrational prejudice and rational exploitation that underlay this policy is well illustrated in the following account of the pogrom of 9–10 November, 1938.*

THE POGROM OF 9–10 NOVEMBER [1938] AND THE DESTRUCTION OF THE ECONOMIC EXISTENCE OF THE JEWS

It is frequently stated that the position of Jews in the German economy was almost unaffected until 1938. But as more recent studies have shown, this was simply not the case. The dis-

SOURCE. Helmut Krausnick and Martin Broszat, *Anatomy of the SS State*, pp. 55–60. Copyright © 1968 by Walker and Company. Reprinted by permission of the publisher, Walker and Company and Collins Publishers, London.

criminatory measures and the boycott must, in general, have had
a directly harmful effect on the economic activities of the Jews.
In addition to the professional restrictions described in the last
chapter, there were also the commercial restrictions, illegal directives and measures affecting various branches of trade (such as
the special trade marks for distinguishing Jewish firms and so
forth) that carried with them either direct or indirect economic
disadvantages for the Jews. The majority of Jews were no longer
able to earn their living; they had no jobs and had to exist, more
or less precariously, on their capital; the Jewish charitable organizations were overwhelmed. Open or veiled threats had already
forced many Jews, particularly in the provinces, to sell their
businesses—nearly always, of course, on unfavourable terms. The
ban on Jews occupying positions of profit (the legality of which
was highly doubtful) and the breaking of business contracts was
not affected by the fact that the "Aryan clause" did not apply to
economic affairs. Not that anyone had any practical objections to
new laws to restrict the economic activities of the Jews; it was
simply that the uncertainties of the existing law sufficed.

Towards the end of 1937 the trend towards the "Aryanization"
of the economy, from which Göring hoped to find the means of
financing the armaments programme, was openly stepped up.
[This was stimulated by the totally unjust expropriation policy
carried out after the *Anschluss* in Austria, where the proprietors
of Jewish undertakings had been removed and replaced by completely unqualified Party officials.] Corrupt practices of the worst
kind were rife, so much so that *Reichskommissar* Bürckel found
it difficult to carry out the Aryanization of the larger undertakings
(at any rate) without corruption creeping in. To stop Jews
handing over their firms to Aryans on a nominal basis, an "Order
(22 April 1938) for the Prevention of Camouflaged Assistance to
Jewish Undertakings" [*Verordnung gegen die Unterstützung der
Tarnung jüdische Gewerbebetriebe*] threatened any German national who lent himself to such practices with imprisonment or
a fine. The way in which the position of the Jews in the economic life of the country was going to be dealt with was clearly
foreshadowed by the "Order for the Disclosure of Jewish Assets"
[*Verordnung zur Anmeldung des Vermögens von Juden*] of 26
April 1938—especially when Göring decreed that a deposit (representing a proportion of the assets) was to be paid as a "guaran-

tee," in the interests of the German economy. Simultaneously it was decreed that special authorization was to be obtained for every sale or lease of land, of an industrial undertaking or of forestry concessions in which Jews were involved, as well as for the opening of any new factory or workshop by a Jew. Jewish industrial undertakings already had to be registered and identified under the provisions of the third order (14 June 1938) of the Reich Citizenship Act. The "Changes in the Industrial Code (German Reich) Act" (6 July 1938) [*Gesetz zur Änderung der Gewerbeordnung für das Deutsche Reich*] finally placed a complete ban on Jews engaging in certain occupations, such as dealing in real estate, acting as caretakers and negotiating loans.

In October 1938, after the Munich Conference, there was a marked increase in Göring's activities. In a speech on the "Four-Year Plan" in the Reich Ministry of Aviation on 14 October 1938, he demanded that the Jewish problem "be tackled energetically and forthwith," and the Jews "must be driven out of the economy." This was now a burning issue for the extreme anti-Semites in the Party. It was difficult to see how a decisive blow against the economic position of the Jews could be struck within the framework of the existing disbarment laws. Yet while they were still active in the economy the total exclusion of the Jews from German life could never be achieved. After Munich the decision on what action to take hung fire; some outside pretext was awaited.

This was supplied by the assassination of the legation secretary, von Rath, by the 17-year old Jew, Grünspan, in Paris on 7 November. "Obviously," wrote the *Völkischer Beobachter* on the very day of the incident, "the German people will be able to draw their own conclusions from this new outrage." On the evening of 9 November, the Reich Minister for Propaganda, Dr Goebbels, lit the fuse. In a rabble-rousing speech to the Party and SS leaders assembled in the *Altenrathaus* in Munich for their annual celebration of 9 November 1923, he unleashed the Jewish pogrom. Known as the *Reichskristallnacht* [Crystal Night]—a title which today has a somewhat euphemistic ring, but was intended as bitter irony by the Berliners who invented it—this has been a stain on the name of Germany ever since. The cunning way in which Goebbels kindled the flame without giving any direct orders can be seen from the official report of the Party

High Court [*Obersten Parteigerichts*] to Göring, in which it was
stated: "The words of the head of the Reich Ministry of Propaganda left the assembled party leaders in no doubt that they were
not to appear openly as the instigators of the demonstrations,
although, of course, they were to organize them and see that
they were carried through." Hitler himself also knew what was
happening—more, he was actually responsbile for the ostensible
"spontaneous reaction of the German people"—although he remained strategically in the background. That Hitler's was the
intellect behind the outbreak has not only been testified by the
then head of the Reich press and others in the know; the support
that he gave to Goebbels's hints to the Party and the SS points in
the same direction. And there is clear evidence in the further
statement in the Party high court report: "After listening to his
[Goebbels's] speech the Führer decided that the demonstrations
to which he had referred ought neither to be prepared nor
organized by the party. On the other hand, if they occurred
spontaneously, nothing was to be done to break them up."
Thereupon synagogues throughout the length and breadth of
Germany were burnt to the ground and over 7,000 Jewish shops
were destroyed. On top of that a fine, originally of one billion,
but eventually amounting to a total of one and a quarter billion
marks, was imposed on thc Jews and the insurance payments to
which they were entitled in compensation for the damage caused
was confiscated by the State. On 11 November Heydrich sent a
telegram to Göring reporting the death of 36 Jews—a later
reckoning by the Party high court made the total 91 dead. The
perpetrators went scot free—unless they had committed "race
pollution" or had overstepped the bounds of "discipline." The
explanation given by the Party courts for this kid-glove treatment was that a remark by Goebbels had forced them to the conclusion that the individual perpetrator "had acted in accordance
with the real wishes of the leadership, however vaguely this may
have been expressed." The lie was also given to the pretence of
spontaneity in the demonstrations by a teletype message sent at
the time by the SS, who were involved only as supplementary
control forces in the disturbances organized at the instigation of
Goebbels by the Party and the SA, and on the whole had very
little to do; they were critical of Goebbels and his machinations
in private, but only because noisy outbreaks of this kind were in

direct contradiction to their well-tried practice of silent, bureaucratic terror. Because of this they dedicated themselves with that
much more zeal to the business of arrests (which came exclusively
within their sphere of jurisdiction), the aim and outcome of
which was the incarceration of some 30,000 particularly wealthy
Jews in concentration camps. The result was a speeding-up of
the emigration programme, since when these Jews were (relatively quickly) released, they left Germany in much greater
numbers than before. "I have not yet met a single German from
any walk of life," wrote the British Chargé d'Affaires in Berlin on
16 November 1938, "who does not disapprove to some degree of
what has occurred. But I fear that not even the unequivocal
condemnation of professed National Socialists and senior officers
in the armed forces will have any effect on the gang of madmen
who are at present in control in Nazi Germany."

At a conference held at the Ministry of Aviation on 12 November 1938 and attended by all those ministers and civil servants
responsible for putting into effect (in accordance with Hitler's
instructions) the policy for excluding the Jews from the economy,
Göring, as chairman, explained that he had been instructed by
Hitler, both verbally and in writing, to "centralize the decisive
step now to be taken" in regard to the Jewish question. In his
speech he referred to the regulations already in operation and to
the final plans for the Aryanization of, first of all, retail shops
and then of factories and partnerships. Göring said that he was
"displeased" with the demonstrations, and must condemn "senseless physical destruction" in all its forms. He then brought up
the question (he had already mentioned it on 14 October) of
forcing the Jews into ghettos. Heydrich, while suggesting "restricted areas" and hinting that the Jews might be made to wear
some distinguishing mark, showed that he really preferred the
idea of a massive emigration programme. Goebbels put forward
the idea of banning Jews from the theatre and cinema as well as
from holiday resorts, swimming pools and so forth. Very little
was heard during all this from the "middle-class" Ministers and
State Secretaries.

A veritable torrent of discriminatory orders then began to
flow over the heads of the Jews. In addition to provisions for
the closing and compulsory sale of Jewish undertakings [wholly
or in part against government stock!] and of real estate belonging

to Jews, these included the exclusion of all Jews from German schools and universities, the designation of restricted areas, the ban on visits to theatres, concert halls, museums, sports stadia, swimming pools and so forth, and the withdrawal of driving licences and licences for commercial vehicles. The seventh order under the Reich Citizenship Act, issued on 5 December 1938, reduced the pensions payable to compulsorily retired Jewish officials; the eighth order (17 January 1939) barred their professions to Jewish dentists, veterinary surgeons and chemists, degrading the first-named into "dental orderlies" qualified only to treat Jewish patients. Finally an order of 21 February 1939 required Jews to surrender all the gold and silver objects in their possession (with the exception of wedding rings) as well as all their precious stones and pearls "for sale by public auction" within a fortnight. A further order of 30 April 1939 revoked the law for the protection of tenants, and it became common practice to force the Jews into what were called "communal Jewish houses." Jews who were fit for work were more and more frequently conscripted for forced labour. After the outbreak of war came the curfew and the confiscation of radio sets (without compensation, of course). This was followed in 1940, among other things, by the withholding of clothing coupons and the severing of telephone connexions. Daily it became more and more obvious that the anti-Jewish regulations were increasingly motivated purely by spite. To what depths of depravity the Party press had sunk since the *Kristallnacht* can nowhere be seen more clearly than in an article in the *Schwarze Korps* of 24 November 1938. After observing scornfully that the "desperate straits" in which the Jewish "parasites" would find themselves would probably mean that "they would turn, as one man, to crime," it concluded with self-righteous hypocrisy: "If this should happen we shall be faced with the stern necessity(!) of rooting out the Jewish underworld in the interest of law and order, just as we root out ordinary criminals: with fire and the sword. Then we shall see the final and utter collapse of Judaism in Germany—its total destruction."

17 FROM   *Alexander Dallin*
German Policy in Russia, 1941–1945

The policy of conquest and colonization in the East for the sole benefit of "the German Reich and People," that Hitler had alluded to in his address to the generals on 3 February 1933, was put into effect after 1939.

ECONOMIC POLICY: NAZI AIMS AND OUTLOOK

"In terms of long-range economic policy, the newly occupied Eastern territories shall be exploited from colonial points of view and with colonial methods."—GÖRING, directive, November 8, 1941

German Economic Goals. The constant and barely concealed German aim for the Eastern economy was to exploit it for the benefit of the Reich. This aim shaped both the long-range plans of colonization and the short-term feeding of Eastern resources into the German war machine. At no time were the interests of the indigenous population given serious consideration. The yardstick of policy in the East, Berlin decreed in its basic economic directives, was "the welfare of the German Reich and People."

The traditional German outlook on the complementary economic roles of an industrial Germany and an agrarian Russia had left its mark on the blueprints drawn up in 1941. In contrast with earlier schemes based on reciprocity, however, the approach —exploiting Eastern agriculture and banishing industry from Russia—amounted to pure colonialism. As a leading official of the Ostministerium put it, the East would supply Europe with raw materials, and in return Germany would ship manufactured goods to the East.

These goals were not entirely conditioned by the Nazi view of

SOURCE. Alexander Dallin, *German Rule in Russia, 1941–1945,* pp. 305–311. Reprinted by permission of St Martin's Press, Inc., The Macmillan Company of Canada and Macmillan London and Basingstoke.

Russia alone. The *Grossraum* concept restricted the economic functions of "inferior" areas—and these included Poland, Yugoslavia, Rumania, and others in addition to the U.S.S.R.—to the more rudimentary processes, primarily to extractive branches of economy: agriculture, mining, and raw materials. The transparent political aim of this approach was to retain the more highly developed forms of economic life, particularly heavy industry and control of finances, at the hub of power, Germany.

While steadfastly refusing to "integrate" the Russian nation into the European political community, Hitler insisted on "integrating" the Eastern economy into that of Europe so as to make its resources available to the West.

"Formerly [the Führer maintained] it would have been impossible for a large state with almost unlimited resources to exist in Eastern Europe . . . while densely populated Central and Western Europe lack raw materials, which they must import from overseas. We must therefore completely open up the territories of the European East, so rich in raw materials, to the highly populated areas of the European West."

In return, Hitler speculated, Russia would provide a vast market for German products. After the war, European industry "would no longer need any foreign markets" because the Soviet population "lives on so low a standard that all industrial products, beginning with the simplest waterglass, could be marketed there." Official plans therefore foresaw that "the occupied Eastern territories [would] always be available to the West as an outlet for products requiring intensive labour. . . ."

Germany's benefits from the Eastern economy were to go even further. "My plan," Hitler told his associates, "is that we should take profits on whatever comes our way." In this future scheme of things, Soviet industry had no *raison d'être*. A de-industrialization (or "naturalization") policy would redound to the Reich's political and economic advantage in that

". . . (1) it prevents the politically undesirable concentration of the native population in industrial centres; (2) the production and utilization of products of intense labour remain with the Reich and the old industrial countries of Europe, assuring them of a satisfactory standard of living."

The bulk of Soviet industry was destined, in the long run, either to be destroyed or, as Hitler suggested on one occasion, to be transferred to the West. If the East was no longer "primitive" and "agrarian," it had to be made so. Where theory and reality diverged, facts were to be changed to conform with dogma.

The Demands of the Hour. While quest for economic gain had not been the most compelling motive for Hitler's attack on the Soviet Union, to the men concerned with the economic exploitation of the East the immediate demands for grain, oil, and raw materials were the alpha and omega of Germany's occupation policy. The members of the economic staffs responsible for the utilization of Eastern resources were neither diplomats of the old school nor ivory-tower economists, nor, finally, dogmatic extremists. Coldly collecting and analysing facts, the war economists calculated months before the invasion that the Soviet territory west of the so-called "AA" (Archangel-Astrakhan) line would suffice to compensate for most German shortages during the balance of the war.

According to them—and the entire economic-administrative edifice from Göring down—long-range political plans (whether of the Bormann or the Rosenberg variety) were subordinate to the urgent economic demands of the war:

"The immediate goal, having top priority . . . for the newly occupied Eastern territories, is to win the present war, to which the Eastern territories must contribute extensively by securing the independence of Europe in food and raw materials. This immediate goal has priority even when occasionally a measure necessary for the prosecution of the war is in conflict with intentions for the future shaping of the *Ostraum*."

The conflict between dogma and practice was recognized in the domain of economics earlier than in some other areas. Maximum exploitation meant the neglect of long-range political and economic transformations which Berlin proposed to carry out. "For the duration of the war the demands of the war economy are the supreme law of all economic activity in the newly occupied Eastern territories." Reluctantly Rosenberg and his staff had to recognize the cogency of this argument.

German needs were particularly acute in agriculture. "According to the orders of the Führer, all measures must be taken which are necessary for the *immediate and maximum exploitation* of the occupied areas in favour of Germany." In 1939 Germany's grain reserves had totalled about seven million tons; by 1941 they had shrunk considerably, though under the terms of the commercial treaty of 1940 the Soviet Union had undertaken to deliver sizeable quantities in the following year. On the eve of the invasion the economic planners expected the armies in the East to live off the land and counted on amassing some seven million tons of grain a year from the future German East. An increase in productivity of 10 or 20 per cent, Berlin anticipated not unrealistically, should not prove an insuperable task; it would suffice to make up the deficit for German-controlled Europe. What mattered above all was neither quality of grains nor the future structure and social relations on the farm but sheer quantity of produce and efficiency in collection—a thesis well in line with the over-all outlook upon the East."

In agriculture the immediate demands of the war economy did not initially necessitate a radical re-thinking of German long-range plans: both pointed towards maximum production and collection. In other branches of economy the conflict between short-term and ultimate goals was more striking. For the needs of the moment it was imperative to resort to "maximum exploitation of the relatively limited means of production"—even in industry—rather than let them wither for political reasons. It was not necessary, however, to restore all branches of Soviet industry, trade, and mining. "It would be utterly erroneous to maintain that we must uniformly pursue the line that all enterprises in the occupied territories are speedily to be put in order and restored. . . . The use of industry may be resumed only in branches where there are shortages."

The urge for all-out, immediate exploitation led to the utilization of resources and facilities with a minimum of organizational and administrative change. It was simplest to postpone such problems as reprivatization and decentralization, and to avoid issues of organizational revamping—unless they bore directly on productive capacity. Thus it was, above all, the economic-minded among the German planners who urged that after the seizure of the East the *status quo* be maintained as the line of least resistance and effort. Even before the invasion they prevailed upon Rosenberg to order all economic enterprises in the East to carry on after the German occupation just as they had under Soviet rule. The Soviet price scale was to be retained, as was most of the administrative machinery on the local level. And so, more crucially, was the entire agrarian system of state and collective farms: *any* change was expected to entail a breakdown, or at least a serious disruption of agricultural production. Promptly, a second argument appeared favouring the maintenance of the *status quo* in agriculture: the state farm and collective farm system permitted more efficient control and collection of produce than would a galaxy of individual households to be created on the ruins of the Soviet system. Hence the directives of May 1941 declared bluntly:

"The premise for [maximum] production and the seizure [*Erfassung*] of surpluses is the maintenance of large enterprises (collective farms and state farms). . . . A splitting into several million peasant economies would make the exertion of German influence on production utopian. Every effort to dissolve the large [agrarian] units must therefore be fought tooth and nail."

The economic staffs willed that the collective farms must serve the Germans as they had the Soviet regime. The aspirations of the Soviet peasantry were of no consequence.

The Geopolitics of Starvation. The defence of the *status quo* thus became the common denominator both of the political officials in their dogmatic resistance to popular aspirations in the East, and of the economic-minded who gave absolute priority to immediate exploitation. Here was the point of intersection between the courses pursued by Koch and Göring. For a variety of reasons, Rosenberg, engrossed as he was in his plans of political gerrymander and racial engineering, could not long abide by this outlook. His clash with the economic exploiters was hastened by their rejection of his policy of national "differentiation."

Both Rosenberg and the economic staffs agreed in assigning special importance to the Ukraine and the Caucasus. But while Rosenberg urged a privileged political status for these areas, the economic staffs proceeded with their plans for the ruthless utilization of Ukrainian grain and Caucasian oil. A policy of special favours clashed with a policy of special burdens. The conflict was never resolved in practice. On paper it was composed by agreeing to the priority of German over indigenous interests and to the disregard of the needs of "deficit" areas. Food consumption in the East was to be reduced so that Germany could obtain the margin. "This fact is the cornerstone on which our measures and economic policy are to be built."

As agreed upon by the economic agencies and the Rosenberg office, the plan in substance called for a division of the "East" into two zones: the forest regions and the black-soil areas.

"Our task in reincorporating [the Soviet economy] . . . into Europe means tearing asunder the present economic balance within the U.S.S.R. . . . The treatment will have to vary according to the types of areas [*Landstriche*]. Only those areas will have to be furthered economically and urgently kept in order which can provide significant food and oil reserves for us."

The rich southern surplus region, which was almost coterminous with Rosenberg's Greater Ukraine, rather than feeding the rest of the Soviet Union, "must in the future turn its face to Europe." As for the "superfluous" north, except to provide for the troops stationed there (Berlin stated a month before the invasion), "Germany has no interest in preserving the productive power of these regions." More than that, the directive ordered that any "shipment of food from the fertile south to the north must be blocked."

"The population of the [northern] regions, especially the urban, will have to look forward to the severest famine. It will be essential to drive the population into Siberia."

It was not that the war economists were so preoccupied with the prospect of collecting tons of grain and herds of cattle that they overlooked the humans living in these areas. With striking frankness they weighed the alternatives and concluded:

"Efforts to save the population from starving to death by bringing in surplus food from the black-soil region [to the northern areas] can be made only at the expense of feeding Europe. They undermine Germany's ability to hold out in the war and to withstand the blockade [imposed by Britain]. There must be absolute clarity on this point. [From this fact] . . . there follows forcibly the extinction of industry as well as of a large percentage of the human beings in the hitherto deficit areas [of Russia]."

The courses suggested by economic and political extremism proved to be identical.

18 FROM *Heinrich Himmler*
On SS Morality and on SS Achievement

The chief instrument in the "administration" of the Eastern territories and of the "final solution of the Jewish question" was the SS. Here are two brief excerpts from a speech made in Poznan on 4 October 1943 by its head, Heinrich Himmler, at a conference of high ranking SS officers, which indicates the SS's attitude towards its "tasks."

ON THE ETHICS OF THE SS

There is one principle which has to be absolutely binding for an SS man: we must be honest, decent, loyal and comradely to members of our own race—and to no one else. How the Russians fare, how the Czechs fare, is a matter of complete indifference to me. What other peoples may possess in the way of good stock of our own sort we shall grab for ourselves, if necessary by stealing their children and raising them ourselves. Whether other peoples live well or die of hunger interests me only insofar as we need them as slaves for our culture; apart from that I couldn't care less. Whether 10,000 Russian females collapse from exhaustion in the construction of a tank trench concerns me only to the extent that the tank trench is completed for Germany. We will never be cruel and heartless where it isn't necessary, that goes without saying. We Germans, who are the only ones in the world to treat animals decently, are also going to have a decent attitude towards these human animals. But it is a crime against our own flesh and blood to worry ourselves about them and to teach them ideals which will only make them the more troublesome to our children and our grandchildren. If someone comes to me and says, "I can't use these children or these women to build a tank trench; it's in-

SOURCE. Walther Hofer, *Der Nationalsozialismus; Dokumente 1933–1945,* pp. 113–114. Copyright 1957 Fischer Bucherei KG, Frankfurt am Main. Reprinted by permission of S. Fischer Verlag.

human, because they will die in the process"—then I can only tell him, "You are a murderer of your own flesh and blood, because if the tank trench isn't built, German soldiers will die, and they are sons of German mothers. They are our flesh and blood." This is what I meant to instill in the SS and, as I believe, have succeeded in instilling in it, as one of the most sacred laws of the future: our concern, our duty is to our people, to our race; that is what we have to care about and to think about, to work for and to fight for, that and nothing else. Everything else is a matter of indifference to us.

ON ONE OF THE ACHIEVEMENTS OF THE SS

I am now referring to the deportation of the Jews, to the extermination of the Jewish people. It is one of those things that is easily said. Every party member says, "The Jewish people is to be exterminated. Of course. Part of our program. Elimination of the Jews. Extermination. We'll do it." And then they all come running, those wonderful 80 million Germans, and every one of them has his good Jew. Of course, of course, the others are all swine, but this one is a top-notch Jew. The people who talk like that—not one of them has witnessed it, not one of them has seen it through. Most of you know what it's like when 100 corpses lie side by side, or 500 corpses or 1000 corpses. To have seen this [job] through and to have remained decent human beings (apart from a few instances of human weakness), that is what has made us tough. It is a glorious page in our history, a page that is and will always remain unwritten.

19 FROM *The Nuremberg Trials*
German Industry Adjusts to New Realities

German industry took full advantage of raw materials and slave labor made available by Nazi conquests. The location of work camps near the concentration and extermination camp Auschwitz was decided on by directors of I. G. Farben *(Germany's largest chemical concern), because natural resources needed for the production of artificial rubber* (Buna) *were available in the area, and because the concentration camp could supply the requisite manpower. The work camps were constructed and run by* I. G. Farben, *with the assistance of SS guards. The German civilians responsible for this operation were not unmindful of the differences between "the working methods of a concentration camp of a free enterprise," but they adjusted ably to the new realities.*

WEEKLY REPORT NO. 11 FOR THE PERIOD
3–9 AUGUST

Preliminary Report. Various conferences with the commandant and his assistants about the assignment of inmates have taken place. As you know, the assignment of two more guard companies have been refused. Through the intervention of the Reichsfuehrer SS, it has now been ordered that all concentration camps are to detach 75 guards for duty at Auschwitz. Of this number, 40 have already arrived during the week covered by this report. In this way, it is possible for the concentration camp to assign another 1,000 inmates in addition to the 816 already employed at present. Of course, this could not be done from one day to the next. In any case, it was possible to increase the number

SOURCE. Partial Translation of Document NI-14543, Prosecution Exhibit 1985, "Extracts from Farben-Auschwitz Weekly Report No. 11, for the period 3–9 August 1941 . . . ," in *Trials of War Criminals before the Nuernberg Military Tribunals*, Nuernberg, October 1946-April 1949, (Washington, D.C., U.S. Government Printing Office, 1953), Vol. pp. 392–3.

of inmates employed from 800 to 1,000 as of Friday, 8 August 1941. During the course of next week, approximately another 700–800 men are to be assigned, if possible.

The assignment of inmates is causing difficulties, because due to the lack of guards—

1. They can always only be assigned in groups of at least 20 or more. The consequence of this is that, in some places, they are working together so closely that they are hindering each other. That is just a fundamental difference between the working methods of a concentration camp and of a free enterprise. The concentration camp has no need to consider economic principles but in free enterprise this must be done; particularly, when it is a case of firms working at standard rates. This is not always sufficiently taken into consideration and recognized by the officials of the concentration camp.

2. The inmates can only march out in daylight and must return to the camp in daylight. If it is foggy in the morning, the inmates are also not permitted to leave the camp. Therefore it is not possible to employ the inmates on shift work; they can only be considered for the day shift.

The conditions will naturally improve once the construction site has been fenced in. The preparations for this have been made so that the fencing can be done by the end of the month. It is now planned to use concrete posts, which are being made in the concentration camp, and barbed wire and wire netting, which we are obtaining from the wire drawing mill in Gleiwitz.

We have furthermore drawn the attention of the officials of the concentration camp to the fact that, in the last few weeks, the inmates are being severely flogged on the construction site by the Capos in increasing measure, and this always applies to the weakest inmates who really cannot work harder. The exceedingly unpleasant scenes that occur on the construction site because of this are beginning to have a demoralizing effect on the free workers (Poles), as well as on the Germans. We have therefore asked that they should refrain from carrying out this flogging on the construction site and transfer it to the inside of the concentration camp.

*   *   *   *   *   *   *   *

[Stamp]

Buna Auschwitz
  Dr. Ambros
  Dr. Buetefisch/Dr. v. Staden
  Santo
  Dr. Mach
  Dr. Eisfeld
  Dr. Duerrfeld
  Faust
  Heidebroek
  [Handwritten] Certified Engineer Rasch

20 FROM *Heinz Lubasz*
 Hitler's Opportunity State

There was a good deal of Nazi talk about revolution, talk which has sometimes been taken seriously by historians and social scientists in their endeavors to identify the nature of fascism in general and of Nazism in particular. The following brief essay takes issue with the view that Hitler made a revolution and suggests that such changes as were made in Germany were merely incidental to the creation of a predatory warfare society.

Hitler, as every schoolboy ought to know, made no revolution, political, economic, or social. He left the old establishment in its entrenched positions in the economy, army, and the state. He erected, at the side of the old establishment, a new, predominantly middle-class, Nazi establishment, with its own bureaucracies, armies, even its own economic enterprises. He corralled the working man by smashing his economic and political organiza-

SOURCE. Heinz Lubasz, "Hitler's Welfare State," in *The New York Review of Books*, Vol. XI, Number 11, December 19, 1968, pp. 33–34. Copyright 1968 The New York Review. Reprinted with permission from *The New York Review of Books*. The article has been revised by the author for the present volume.

tions, and subordinating him to the joint authority of his employer and the new Nazi Labor Front. He then coordinated and mobilized the whole into that predatory and dynamic warfare society whose glorious national mission—the subjugation and exploitation of non-German (or, rather, "non-Aryan") populations —was to become the cornerstone of Hitler's grand design and the substitute for the revolution he never made.

We know that Hitler came to power with the help of bankers, industrialists, and Junker politicians, on the understanding that he would convert the mass of the population to the "national" cause. He had already captured about a third of the population, and it seemed likely that he could win all of it. The old elites expected him to "discipline" the political parties, "tame" the unions, throw out the "Marxists" (which meant social democrats as well as communists), and build up a powerful military-industrial machine to get Germany moving again.

Still, if this was not a revolution, it wasn't precisely a counter-revolution either, certainly not merely a counter-revolution. The old establishment remained, but it had little power. The magnates who "hired" Hitler soon discovered that they had collaborated with him. They had in fact entered into a fluid, ill-defined partnership in which Hitler quickly made himself the senior partner and eventually the undisputed boss.

What began as a cynical but comparatively sedate *mariage de convenance* ended up as a wild joint venture in mass destruction, far wilder and far more destructive than the plotters among the old elites had bargained for. They had hoped, many of them, for something like the comparatively static fascism of Mussolini. Some had even dreamed of a monarchical fascism under a restored Kaiser (Thyssen was among those dreamers). But they had miscalculated. They found themselves stuck with the plebeian pseudo-revolutionary, the rabble-rousing fanatic whom most of them privately despised. They had wanted to use him, and continued to do so. Hitler in his turn used them, taking them moreover in a direction they would almost certainly not have chosen themselves.

Thus it happened that, while men with university degrees continued to run the machinery of state, men with aristocratic titles continued to run the army, and men of wealth and polish continued to own and operate the economy, the uneducated, un-

couth, lower-middle-class Hitler was the real boss. The old establishment did well for itself out of the partnership. But it did not,
in the last resort, control it. What is more, it had to countenance
the rise of the partly fanatical, partly careerist following with
which the Führer now proceeded to build the new Nazi establishment.

For Hitler did not arrive alone. He brought with him a virtual
army of kindred spirits, the predominantly middle-class and lower
middle-class faithful who largely comprised the Nazi movement.
Like their Führer, they had been clamoring for office, for opportunity, for a place in the sun. These men of the social and
economic middle—shopkeepers, artisans, schoolteachers, petty
officials, peasants—had wanted to strike out against both the
classes above them and the classes below them, against the capitalists with their trusts and department stores and against the
industrial workers with their unions, against their social superiors
and their social inferiors. For Nazism as a movement was the
would-be rebellion of the distressed and disgruntled in-between
classes.

World War I had hit many of these people particularly hard in
various ways; as did the postwar years. The war had been fi-
nanced largely out of middle-class savings. First the war was
lost, and then the savings as well. Many veterans had found the
"meaning" of their existence in fighting for Germany. In the
postwar society—with the war lost, the Kaiser gone, the Social
Democrats in the government, and few jobs to be had—they were
bored, restless, bitter; they found themselves living in a society
drastically different from the one they had fought for, and worse.
Many veterans—and many non-veterans—identified their feelings
of defeat with the nation's defeat, the nation's former glory with
the good old days when middle-class people still counted for
something and could make a decent living.

Hitler promised to set everything right again: defeat—individual *and* national—would be avenged and turned into victory;
capitalism would be curbed and so would the unions; all Germans would be united once more under a single leader in
honorable and soldierly service to the national cause. The people
would rise in triumph, through discipline, will power, and combat, to vanquish their enemies, rid Germany of the nefarious
Jews, and assert the superior rights belonging to a superior race.

All this and much more went to make up the ideological mish-mash of the Nazi movement. This was the "program" of the Nazi "revolution."

The point to notice is that this "revolutionary" program con-sisted from the first of a mixture of aims: social reform plus militarization plus national self-assertion. It was these three strands taken together, and not merely a plan for the reconstruc-tion of society, which caught the imagination of so many Ger-mans. Hitler and his "revolution" stood for all three. When the Führer finally did come to power he could so easily scrap the vague and inconsistent plans for social reform precisely because he was in deadly earnest about the other two "planks" in his "platform." Moreover, militarization and national self-assertion under Nazi auspices meant the creation of a predatory warfare society which provided jobs, uniforms, medals. The social revolu-tion that had been promised never came. But the warfare society did, and *it* provided the opportunities. It was not revolution but war and preparation for war, militarization, and, later on, the fruits of victory which provided the Nazified middle class with material and psychological rewards.

In the new establishment Hitler gave his followers new oppor-tunities and a new sense of importance and well-being. In the Labor Front which controlled the working classes, in the Reich Food Estate which controlled the farmers, in the various Party organs, and especially in the SS—police, army, colonial ad-ministration, and economic enterprise all rolled into one—the Nazified members of the middle classes found countless oppor-tunities. A few even managed to infiltrate the strongholds of the old establishment, but they did not get very far: few Nazis reached ministerial level, few became generals, very few indeed became company directors. Their best chances by far lay in the new establishment.

The predatory warfare society which Hitler created was in fact a new and thoroughly perverse kind of opportunity state. For those industries which were needed for war, preeminently the chemical industry (in which I.G. Farben attained to fantastic heights in foreign acquisitions and profits); for those loyal hench-men who got jobs entailing official and unofficial perquisites; for the many loyal followers who were able to acquire, for a pittance, first Jewish and then foreign factories, shops, farmsteads, etc.;

and even for the workers who had to be paid if they were to work, and for whom there was now plenty of work to be done; for all these there were material rewards, even if the rewards were unequally distributed. There was also psychological rewards for those—and they were many—who got a sense of uplift, of excitement, of togetherness, indeed of revived national vitality and dignity—from the dynamic way in which Nazi Germany presented itself to itself: through flags, parades, speeches, emblems, spectacles; through pseudo-Wagnerian Reichsparteitage; through the exhortations and self-congratulations of press, film and radio; through these vehicles and others Nazi Germany generated the sense of a people on the way to a better future. It was not impossible to believe that a bright new day was dawning for Germany, to feel that somehow one was now, or one's children soon would be, better off.

And all of this the Nazis accomplished without any revolutionary changes in the actual structure of economy or society—except for their treatment of the "inferior" Jews and, later on, the "inferior" Slavs.

This exception, in fact, goes far to explain how it was possible for things to have got better in the absence of the revolution that was first promised as indispensable and then abandoned as superfluous, or as having already taken place. Three days after becoming chancellor Hitler outlined the "solution" to Germany's economic problems in an address to the principal officers of the army and the navy: the problem was underemployment and underproduction, too many people for too few jobs, and to few markets for Germany's products. The answer was: rearmament, which would stimulate production and decrease unemployment; and the forcible colonization of Eastern Europe, which would yield land, raw materials, markets, an outlet for surplus population, territories to exploit, and (he might have added) people to maltreat. For nothing so generates a sense of superiority and well-being than the systematic degradation of others.

The exploitation and degradation of "non-Aryans" was in fact the material and psychological substitute for the social revolution Hitler never made. In enormous measure, the material and "spiritual" rewards Hitler was able to offer the Germans—for a while, at least—depended precisely on the victimization of "alien populations." The fate of these victims—principally Jews at first, then mainly Slavs, but in the end people from all over conquered Europe—was an integral part of the Nazi social program, an essential part of its social system. By contrast with the program for social reform, it was consistently and rigorously carried out. It involved—for those Jewish Germans excluded from German society, for the concentration-camp inmates and prisoners of war all races and nationalities who were worked to death, and for those simply exterminated—a "status revolution" incomparably more drastic than any experienced by "Aryan" Germans.

Thanks to Hitler, Germany avoided both revolution and reform, and yet established an—admittedly short-lived—welfare state of sorts. While it lasted, Germans reaped the material and psychological rewards. It was the "non-Aryan" victims who paid the price.

PART THREE

Japan's "Imperial Way"

21 FROM *Richard G. Storry*
The Rise of Japanese Fascism

The beginnings of fascism in Japan may be dated from Kita Ikki's Plan for the Reorganization of Japan (see below, Number 23) of 1919. Thereafter, numerous groups and programs of a fascist bent came to the fore. But it was not until the depression of the early 1930s and the "Manchurian Incident" of 1931 that fascism took firm institutional root—in sections of the Japanese army. The climax of insurgent militarist nationalism came with the so-called "February Twenty-Sixth Incident" of 1936.

On February 26th, 1936, the world was startled by the news that part of the Japanese Army had mutinied and had seized important buildings in the centre of Tokyo, after having murdered several men in public life. When loyal troops were massed to suppress the rebellion, it seemed inevitable that severe fighting would break out. Yet within the space of four days the mutineers surrendered without bloodshed, and life in Tokyo returned to normal.

The underlying cause of this remarkable outbreak was the rivalry that had developed during the previous four years be-

SOURCE. Richard G. Storry, "Fascism in Japan," *History Today*, November 1956, pp. 717–726. Reprinted by special permission of Richard G. Storry. The article has been revised by the author for the present volume.

tween two politically active factions in the Japanese Army. These were called the *Kodo-ha* and *Tosei-ha*. Their mutual struggle was quite unknown to the mass of the Japanese people at the time; it was indeed hidden, to some extent, from the eyes of experienced foreign observers in Tokyo. Even today, after the publication of several memoirs and other works in Japanese dealing with the subject, the full story of what took place on February 26th, 1936, and of what lay behind the revolt, remains undisclosed.

The *Kodo-ha* took its name from the concept of *Kodo*, "the Imperial Way," popularized by the voluble General Sadao Araki while he was Minister of War in 1932 and 1933. *Kodo* is not easily explained. Its advocates often claimed that it was ineffable. But it may be summed up, rather inadequately perhaps, as the ideal of perfect loyalty and self-surrender to the Emperor. It was an ideal embracing the belief that if all political and economic power were placed in the Emperor's hands every domestic and foreign difficulty would be overcome. The concept was in essence mystical; but it included, in so far as it had a practical application, a strong element of national socialism. This had been preached for some years by a former Black Dragon Society adventurer, Ikki Kita, who advocated the nationalization of land, of large manufacturing and mining industries, banks and shipping. Kita was at once anti-capitalist and pro-imperialist. A great admirer of the Imperial House and of the armed forces, he declared that Japan was "a proletarian among the nations," and had therefore a natural right to share the resources held by such "capitalists among the nations" as Soviet Russia and the British Commonwealth. Kita, in other words, was Japan's first Fascist. His doctrines became increasingly popular among junior army officers as the effects of the World Depression were felt in Japan. A high proportion of officers came from farming districts.[1] They had firsthand knowledge of the hardships that afflicted the peasants from 1930 onwards. Besides the catastrophic fall of the market for raw silk, there was actual famine, in 1934, throughout almost all North-eastern Japan.

---

[1] However a majority of the mutinous officers in Tokyo in February 1936 were in fact the sons of high-ranking military figures. See the excellent study by Ben-ami Shillony, "The February 26 Affair: Politics of a Military Insurrection" in George M. Wilson (ed.), *Crisis Politics in Prewar Japan* (Tokyo, Sophia University Press, 1970), p. 26.

In such circumstances there developed among the younger, and meagrely paid, officers of the army a good deal of radical, and even revolutionary, unrest. Agitation was never directed against the Monarchy. On the contrary, the Monarchy was regarded as the single hope for the future. In the eyes of young officers party politicians were corrupt and self-seeking, the great financial and commercial combines were avaricious and oppressive, the Emperor's own Court advisers timid and weak. Even their own generals often seemed to be tainted by their association with the great capitalists and Diet politicians. On the other hand, the Left-Wing movement was condemned as being unpatriotic and pro-Soviet. Among the young army officers there grew up a demand for the introduction of Kita's programme by the most expeditious means, that of a *coup d'état*. Naturally enough, senior officers were profoundly worried by the political unrest that disturbed the minds of so many of their juniors. But there were some generals who felt a measure of real sympathy with this unrest, and among them two were outstanding. They were Generals Araki and Mazaki.

From the time of the successful seizure of Manchuria in the autumn of 1931 the Japanese Army played, both overtly and behind the scenes, an increasingly important part in the direction of every phase of national policy; and during the years 1932 and 1933, when Araki was Minister of War, the *Kodo-ha* was the dominant faction in the army. Its position was made all the stronger during this period by the appointment of Mazaki as Inspector-General of Military Education, one of the three chief posts in the army.

The rival faction, the *Tosei-ha*, was equally determined to secure military control of national policy. But this faction contained senior officers, such as Ugaki and Sugiyama, who were prepared to co-operate with the great business houses and their affiliated political parties in the Diet. *Tosei* means "control." The leaders of the *Tosei-ha* had a genuine horror of the radical ideas cherished by many of the junior officers, and they were eager to enforce discipline in the army, to control the restless junior ranks. The *Tosei-ha* had its own extremist fringe, including civilian adventures such as Shumei Okawa; and its patriotism did not exclude the use of terrorist methods. But, broadly speaking, the *Tosei-ha* was more conservative and cautious than the *Kodo-ha*.

One of the issues dividing the two factions was the future direction of Japanese armed expansion abroad. The *Tosei-ha* favoured an advance. South from Manchuria into China. The *Kodo-ha* openly advocated an advance in the other direction, from Manchuria into Siberia and the Maritime Province of which Vladivostock is the capital. During the heyday of this faction General Araki spoke constantly, in public as well as privately, of the great crisis (*kiki*) that must occur in 1935 or 1936, when Japan would be ready to fight the Soviet Union. Such talk alarmed many responsible people in Tokyo, notably Korekiyo Takahashi, Minister of Finance and a former Premier, who fought hard to check the rising military budgets.

In 1934 it was apparent that the *Kodo-ha* was losing ground. Araki resigned at the beginning of the year and the *Tosei-ha* began to martial its forces for the removal of Mazaki from his position as Inspector-General. Finally, in July 1935, Mazaki, much against his will, was compelled to relinquish office. This had one dramatic consequence. On August 12th a lieutenant-colonel named Aizawa walked into the Ministry of War and killed with his sword Major-General Nagata, a very influential figure in the *Tosei-ha* and a known enemy of Mazaki.

Somewhat to his surprise Aizawa was arrested on the spot. He was confined to the quarters in Tokyo of the First Division, and there his court-martial was held. This was accorded considerable publicity in the press. There was much sympathy for the defendant, who gave a passionate dissertation on the sincerity and unselfishness of his motives. The Aizawa trial in fact became a sounding board for the views of the *Kodo-ha*.

By the end of 1935 there were rumours in the capital that discontented officers of the *Kodo-ha* were plotting some kind of *coup d'état*. The rumours were well founded. For late in December some thirty officers of junior rank met at a restaurant in the Shinjuku district of Tokyo to protest against the appointment of Admiral Makoto Saito, an ex-Premier, as Lord Keeper of the Privy Seal—a position of great influence. For the Lord Keeper was the day-to-day adviser to the Emperor, in constant attendance and always present during audiences granted to Ministers of State and high officials. Saito was distrusted by the army, and by the *Kodo-ha* more especially, on the grounds of his alleged moderate and liberal sentiments.

The meeting in Shinjuku was attended by Ikki Kita and by

another civilian fanatic, Zei Nishida, a former army officer. The Minister of War, General Kawashima, heard of the meeting; at which, so it was said, plans were discussed for an armed insurrection. Kawashima seems to have made up his mind to order disciplinary action against the officers concerned.[2] Even if no seditious talk had taken place at the meeting Kawashima would have had good grounds for taking action; for, by a Rescript of the Emperor Meiji, officers and men of the army and navy were expressly forbidden to take any part in political activities. Yet nothing was done.

In the following month, January 1936, a curious episode took place on the border of Manchuria and Siberia. A Japanese detachment of about a hundred officers and men crossed the frontier into Soviet territory. Four officers were killed.[3] The rest were taken prisoner. To this day the circumstances of this affair remain obscure. All news of it was effectively concealed from the public at the time. It is quite possible, however, that the incident was planned to provoke hostilities with Russia, in accordance with the aims of the *Kodo-ha*.

At about the same time the First Division in Tokyo had orders to prepare for a move to Manchuria within a matter of a few weeks. The authorities may well have felt that the sooner this Division was overseas the better, for in January the police arrested one of its officers on suspicion of planning the assassination of General Watanabe, Mazaki's successor as Inspector-General.

On February 20th there was a General Election, in which the Minseito—the rather more liberal of the two main political parties—defeated its chief rival, the Seiyukai. At the same time the *Shakai Taishuto*, "the Social Mass Party," made striking gains, increasing its representation in the Lower House from 3 to 18 members. Some Japanese have suggested that there was a connection between the success of the *Shakai Taishuto* at the polls, although it was still greatly inferior to that of the Minseito, and the outbreak of the mutiny six days later. The *Shakai Taishuto* favoured national socialism and to some extent their agitation expressed the discontent of farmers and soldiers alike. But there can be little doubt that it was the First Division's imminent de-

[2] *Saionji-Harada Memoirs*, Part X, Chapter 193.
[3] *Ibid.*, Chapter 195a.

parture overseas that had a greater bearing on the date chosen for the rising. Ikki Kita, for example, declared that the outbreak was premature.

When the mutiny occurred no officer above the rank of captain took part in it. But it is clear that the leaders of the mutinous detachments, such as Captains Nonaka and Ando, must have received encouragement of some kind, beforehand, from certain of their seniors. Names of generals mentioned in this connection included those of Mazaki, Yanagawa and Kobata. Yet it is on the whole improbable that Mazaki, or any other leader of the *Kodo-ha*, took the initiative in inciting the young officers of the First Division to armed revolt. The embers of insurrection were well alight. The real incendiaries were Ikki Kita, Zei Nishida and two cashiered officers, Muranaka and Isobe.[4] The last two were the go-betweens for funds reaching the mutineers. One ultra-nationalist Kansai businessman is said to have given them a very large sum of money. Another backer seems to have been the Seiyukai politician and shipping magnate, Fusanosuke Kuhara. Some of the funds were the proceeds of virtual blackmail; and Seihin Ikeda, of the great Mitsui concern, appears to have given money under duress. Evidently Kunishige Tanaka, a retired general, and Marquis Yoshichika Tokugawa were in touch with the conspirators; for according to the Commandant of the Tokyo *Kempei* (Military Police) these two "planned to visit the Emperor and report on matters when the insurgent group succeeded."[5] Perhaps they expected to step into the shoes of such senior Palace officials as the Lord Keeper of the Privy Seal and the Grand Chamberlain, who were marked for assassination by the rebels. Later, during the summer of 1936, the Minister of War, General Terauchi, had this to say about the mutiny:—

"It is very distressing. In connection with the February 26th Incident there are those who, although not directly involved, knew that plots were afoot and yet kept quiet. Some directly incited the men to action; others saw this happening and even then kept quiet. A really disgraceful group of men were gathered to-

4 Muranaka and Isobe were involved in an obscure conspiracy in November 1934, known as "The Military Academy Affair." They were cashiered later, for writing a pamphlet criticizing senior officers of the *Tosei-ha*.

5 *Saionji-Harada Memoirs*, Part X, Chapter 210.

gether. And yet if all who were involved resigned it would be difficult to find men to take their places."[6]

Some time before 5 a.m. on February 26th, rather more than 1,400 troops of the 1st and 3rd Infantry Regiments of the First Division left their barracks under the leadership of Captain Shiro Nonaka, a company commander in the 3rd Infantry Regiment. Nonaka's own regimental commander tried in vain to persuade the men to return to their quarters. When he saw that he had failed he committed suicide. The mutineers were joined by about fifty men from the Guards Division. The whole force, of some 1,480 officers and men, represented about 10 per cent of the strength of the Tokyo Garrison, which consisted at that time of six infantry regiments—the four regiments of the Guards Division and two regiments of the First Division (two more regiments of this Division were stationed outside the city).

There was a heavy snowfall that morning, as detachments of troops took possession of a group of buildings—the Ministry of War, the Sanno Hotel and the Metropolitan Police Headquarters —immediately west of the Imperial Palace. Simultaneously parties of mutineers went to the official residence of the Prime Minister, Admiral Keisuke Okada, and to the homes of the Lord Keeper of the Privy Seal (Admiral Saito), the Grand Chamberlain (Admiral Suzuki), the Minister of Finance (Korekiyo Takahashi) and the Inspector-General of Military Education (General Watanabe). Two parties made their way out of the city. One went to the villa by the sea, at Okitsu, of Prince Saionji, the last of the *Genro* ("elder statesmen"); the other went to a small hotspring resort, Yugawara, where Count Makino, Admiral Saito's predecessor as Lord Keeper, happened to be staying.

Of these seven distinguished and, on the whole, elderly victims four survived. Takahashi, Saito and Watanabe were savagely murdered. Admiral Kantaro Suzuki, the Grand Chamberlain, was left for dead. It is said that Captain Teruzo Ando, in charge of the party that attacked the admiral's home, was persuaded by Mrs. Suzuki to depart immediately after Admiral Suzuki fell. Suzuki made an almost miraculous recovery from serious injuries and lived to become the Japanese Premier at the time of the Surrender to the United States in 1945. Old Prince Saionji had warning in time, from the Shizuoka police who took him under their protection. Makino, another old man, probably owed his life to his granddaughter, Kazuko, now Mrs. Aso, the daughter of the post-war Prime Minister, Shigeru Yoshida. When the party of soldiers broke into the inn at which Count Makino was staying he and his grandchild, then aged about nineteen or twenty, made their escape into the grounds at the back. They were ascending a steep slope when they were discovered by the soldiers, and according to one account the girl spread her arms out in front of her grandfather. The soldiers, moved by her courage, did not shoot.[7]

But the most astonishing escape was that of the Prime Minister, Admiral Okada. His brother-in-law, Colonel Matsuo, greatly resembled him in appearance. In the confusion accompanying the attack on the official residence—five police guards were killed defending the building—Colonel Matsuo deliberately exposed himself to the mutineers, who, mistaking him for the Premier, shot him down. Okada concealed himself in a cupboard and many hours later was able to walk out of the house disguised as one of the mourners following what was thought to be the body of the dead Premier.

These acts of violence were accomplished by eight o'clock in the morning, by which time the city lay under a blanket of snow —circumstances that exercised a peculiar appeal for Japanese nationalists of the extreme kind. For two famous acts of bloody revenge in the history of the city had taken place in a blinding snowstorm.

The mutineers set up their headquarters in the Sanno Hotel and then waited for action on the part of those high officers, supposedly sympathetic with them, who would—as it was hoped —take over the reins of government. No cordon was placed round the Imperial Palace. For the mutineers had aimed their activities not against the sacred person of the Emperor but against his "evil counsellors." The passivity of the mutineers, following the

---

[7] Such is the account given by Grew in his *Ten Years in Japan* (pp. 157–8). Hugh Byas in *Government by Assassination* (pp. 121–2) gives a rather different version which indeed may be the true one—namely, that the slope of the hill up which Makino and his granddaughter were climbing was too steep for the use of a machine-gun, which had been brought into play. Byas says that a soldier fired a shot with his rifle and claimed he had killed Makino.

immediate seizure of their group of buildings and the attacks on Okada and the others, seems, on reflection, both striking and curious. Clearly they were waiting for others to move. A Japanese writer has explained the strangely naïve attitude of the mutineers in this way:

"The rebel officers did not go into action in order to establish any particular cabinet or system of government. (Their idea was) Only restore imperial rule and let the light of the nation shine forth; then politics will be put right automatically."[8]

At this juncture the resolution shown by the Emperor proved to be decisive. The absence of Saito and Suzuki meant that action, in the early stages at least, depended largely on the Emperor's personal initiative. "All action was taken" (says a contemporary account) "on His Majesty's own decision."[9] The surviving members of the cabinet made the Palace their rendezvous. Members of the Imperial Family—including the Chiefs of the Army and Navy General Staffs—also gathered at the Palace. Senior army commanders present in Tokyo made the *Kaikosha*, the Army Club, their headquarters. But at this crisis there was a moment, at the very outset, when every eye was turned to the Palace awaiting a sign.

There is a well-known Japanese saying—*kateba kangun*, "if you win you are the imperial army." This could be rephrased as *kangun nara katsu*, "if you are the imperial army you win." As one authority has put it: "In the history of Japanese factional politics, possession of the emperor was nine-tenths of the game."[10] The rebel officers hoped that their effective spokesman in the Palace at this crucial hour would be the Emperor's chief aide-de-camp, General Shigeru Honjo. The latter was a personal friend of Mazaki's and he was also father-in-law of one of the ringleaders of the mutiny, Captain Ichitaro Yamaguchi. Honjo did indeed attempt to defend the aims and motives, if not the actions, of the mutineers when he was summoned to report on the insur-

[8] Tatsuo Iwabuchi, *The Genealogy of the* Gunbatsu, *Chuo Koron*, July 1964.

[9] *Saionji-Harada Memoirs*, Part X, Chapter 196.

[10] John Whitney Hall, "A Monarch for Modern Japan," in Robert E. Ward (Ed.) *Political Development in Modern Japan* (Princeton: Princeton University Press, 1968) p. 44.

rection to the Emperor. In fact, it now seems very probable, to say the least, that both the War Minister, General Kawashima, and certain other officers of the Ministry were prepared to accept the *fait accompli* that morning. At least some members of the Imperial Family, too, appear to have been ready to listen to the demands of the mutineers. It has even been argued, rather convincingly, that *Kodo-ha* generals persuaded the Supreme War Council, meeting on the afternoon of 26 February, to adopt a declaration, to be issued by the War Minister, in support of the rebels' cause.[11]

The Emperor's attitude was made clear at once. He had not the smallest sympathy with those who, professing great loyalty, had butchered old men in their homes. The Emperor referred to the disturbance as a mutiny. "I will give you one hour," he said to the Minister of War, "in which to suppress the rebels." He declined to accept the resignation of the cabinet. He would not consider the question of a new government until the rebels had been put down. His comment on the mutinous officers was direct and uncompromising: "Any soldier who moves Imperial troops without my orders is not my soldier, no matter what excuse he may have."[12]

The navy from the first showed itself ready to take a hand in suppressing the mutiny. Admiral Osumi, the Navy Minister, went to the Palace, soon to be protected by loyal troops of the Guards Division, with an armed escort to bluejackets. The First Fleet was ordered to concentrate in Tokyo Bay, and ratings from the naval base at Yokosuka were brought into the Tokyo port area.

At the same time army reinforcements were called for and most of these had reached Tokyo by the morning of the 27th. Martial Law was now proclaimed and a special Martial Law Headquarters was set up under Lieutenant-General Kashii.

Yet the Martial Law Proclamation, signed by the Emperor on the 27th, did not refer directly to the mutiny, but only to the danger of an outburst by "Communist elements" which was to be suppressed. Moreover, the seeming ambiguity of the phraseology used was such as to give the impression that the mutinous detach-

11 Shillony in Wilson, *op. cit.*, p. 40.
12 *Saionji-Harada Memoirs*, Part X, Chapter 196.

ments had been allotted a role as part of the patrol force under command of Martial Law Headquarters.[13] In fact the Proclamation appeared to confirm an announcement put out by Tokyo Garrison on the evening of the 26th. This declared a state of "wartime defence" (*senji keibi*) and made the First Division responsible for maintaining order. The announcement made no mention of the mutiny.[14] In other words, everything was very much in the balance, so far as the army leaders were concerned. Only the Emperor and the admirals, one might say, were resolute from the beginning in a determination to punish the mutineers.

As time passed the Emperor became more impatient. "Why are the rebels not suppressed by now?" he kept asking the generals when they reported at the Palace.[15] But the army commanders opposed hasty action. The 27th and 28th were days of parley with the rebels, whose leaders met three senior generals—Mazaki, Abe and Nishi—at the official residence of the Minister of War. It is generally admitted that Mazaki finally tried to persuade the mutinous officers to surrender. And later he cited as proof that he had never countenanced the rebellion.

On February 29th it looked as though fighting might start before evening, for early that morning Martial Law Headquarters issued a statement that it had been decided to secure "a settlement by military force." A last-minute manoeuvre, however, was an appeal over the heads of the rebel officers to the rank and file. Lieutenant-General Kashii issued a special order saying that although the rebel non-commissioned officers and men might have acted from pure motives, in obedience to their superiors, they were now under orders from the Emperor to return to their barracks. A simple paraphrase of this order was mimeographed, and copies were dropped on the rebels from aircraft; and an advertisement balloon, bearing the message on a streamer in large ideographs, was hoisted to a height at which it was visible to the mutineers. It was, perhaps, the last sentence of the message that was the most telling. It read: "Your fathers, mothers, brothers and sisters are all weeping because you will become traitors." The straightforward emotional appeal was effective.

[13] Shillony in Wilson, *op. cit.*, p. 41.

[14] *Asahi Shimbun* 27 February 1936.

[15] *Saionji-Harada Memoirs*, Part X, Chapter 196.

The rebel officers felt that the soldiers under their command, bivouacked in the snow round the Sanno Hotel, were *"kawaiso"* ("to be pitied") and they no longer felt able to hold them to an enterprise that had clearly failed.

By midday on the 29th large numbers had surrendered, and indeed the surrender was completed by three o'clock that afternoon. Captain Nonaka shot himself, but Ando and the others gave themselves up. They had decided to stand their trial, in the confident expectation that they would have a chance, like Aizawa, of advocating the ideals of *Kodo* in a blaze of publicity. But they were to be disappointed.

When the surrender had been completed, and the barriers of barbed wire taken down, General Kawashima, Minister of War, gave a statement to the press. In exceptionally strong words he spoke of the mutiny as having left "a blot on the divine reign" of the Emperor. The statement indeed reflected the disgust felt by the Emperor, who was soon to issue a Rescript to the army condemning the military in harsh terms. This Rescript was not made public; it was not even conveyed to the higher ranks of the army. General Terauchi, Minister of War after the mutiny, put it in his drawer at the Ministry where it was found by his successor. Presumably it was too outspoken for publication.

Within a few weeks Mazaki was under interrogation by the *Kempei*. He has always claimed that the mutiny was engineered, at least indirectly, by his enemies in the *Tosei-ha* to discredit him. At all events a case against him could not be proved; and in 1937, thanks to the intervention of Prince Konoye, he was released from custody. The rebel officers were tried and convicted in secret. Thirteen of them were condemned to death and were executed by firing squad on July 13th, six days after the execution of Aizawa. Ikki Kita, Zei Nishida and the two cashiered officers, Muranaka and Isobe, were also tried and condemned in secret; but they were not executed until September 1937.

The mutiny was the climax of revolutionary nationalism in modern Japan. Thereafter the *Tosei-ha* was firmly in the saddle, consolidating its position by using the threat of revolutionary fascism "from below" as a pretext for imposing what was in fact fascism "from above." The triumph of the *Tosei-ha* meant that the next move on the continent would be against China, rather than Russia. This led in turn to deeper commitment and a further advance to the South and so, in the end, to Pearl Harbour.

22 FROM   *Robert A. Scalapino*
          The Triumph of Fascism in Japan

The sequel to the "February Twenty-sixth Incident" was the collapse of what still remained of Japan's liberal-democratic political structure, and its swift replacement by a garrison state structure—by "fascism from above."

The "February Twenty-sixth Incident" was an act of desperation, born of the profound discouragement over the lack of "reform" and the nature of current trends. It would have stood a better chance of success had it been staged earlier. Its failure marked the climax of attempts at revolution by the radical right. Now, men from the Tosei ha moved swiftly and dealt the Kodo ha and allied groups a series of heavy blows. Certain generals having past or present connections with radicals were transferred to the reserves, including Mazaki and Araki. The young leaders of the plot were tried with record speed, and this time a minimum of sentimentality was allowed to pervade the court atmosphere. Thirteen army officers and four civilians, including both Kita and Nishida were executed. From this point on, the radicals had their strongest foothold overseas, where many had already been sent.

At the same time, however, the aftermath of the February Twenty-sixth Incident saw the further development of the garrison state in Japan. With internal friction now reduced, the controlling Tosei men exercised a total power over Japanese politics far greater than that during the Saito-Okada era, and a power which steadily increased. Men like Generals Terauchi Hisaichi, Tojo Hideki, Sugiyama Hajime, and Koiso Kuniaka became powerful figures, both within the army and in the general political scene. The Okada cabinet, and Konoe, whom the Jushin wanted, refused the premiership on grounds of ill health. Then,

SOURCE. Robert A. Scalapino, *Democracy and the Party Movement in Prewar Japan*, pp. 384–392. (Berkeley and Los Angeles, 1953). Originally published by the University of California Press; reprinted by permission of The University of California.

after ascertaining that he would be satisfactory to the military, they turned to former Foreign Minister Hirota Koki. When Hirota began to construct his cabinet, he was presented with a series of army ultimatums on both personnel and policies. One of these demands was that the number of party seats in the cabinet be reduced to two, but since Hirota had to deal with the Diet and had previously promised the major parties two seats apiece, on this one item he held fast and the army finally accepted his demand. Otherwise, however, Hirota gave way on every point and promised also to abide by an army program which included armament expansion, augmented economic controls, and strengthened supervision over "information." When the new Diet convened, moreover, War Minister Terauchi took a more truculent position on the floor than had been seen since World War I. His creed was contained in the demands for a thorough "renovation" of government, the abandonment of "liberalism," and the establishment of a "controlled, unified state." His contempt for the old parties was so open and his browbeating tactics so ruthless that some of the more courageous members of the Diet could not remain silent. This situation finally led to the famous incident in January, 1937, between Hamada Kunimatsu, Seiyukai Diet member, and the Minister of War. Hamada openly accused the military of foisting a dictatorship upon Japan, and in an emotion-laden exchange, the aging Diet member held his ground.

Indeed, in the period of the Hirota cabinet and its successor, the Hayashi cabinet, the parties offered more resistance to the military than at any time since 1932. Behind this resistance lay several important factors. Soon after the February Twenty-sixth Incident the army had expanded its power very abruptly, less hindered by internal problems and less conciliatory toward outside interests. The price of compromise with the military was going up. Although the men of the Tosei faction were not strident revolutionaries and although they continued to be hated by Kodo ha remnants and various radicals, they had adjusted to some of the radical demands. In the army program, there were many planks calculated to bring forth the antagonism of the commercial-industrial groups, and the challenge to any form of representative government was now inescapable. The parties, moreover, were somewhat strengthened by public reactions to the incident of February 26 and by the Emperor's rebuke to the military. The 1936 elections had also provided encouragement.

None of these factors, to be sure, altered the basic weaknesses affecting the parties, nor did they halt the march of military power. The next few months and years saw many changes. One of the earliest was the reëstablishment of the old rule allowing only active-service generals or admirals to serve as minister of war and minister of the navy. But for a brief while, it seemed that the parties and the forces supporting them might be revitalized and take the offensive. There was little unity in Japanese politics in the hectic years of 1936 and early 1937. Even the Seiyukai adopted a hostile position toward the Hirota government, and in the aftermath of Hamada's attack, Terauchi resigned and the cabinet fell. The Jushin helpfully nominated Ugaki, who had long been close to the Minseito and now represented the most conservative element within the army, a man who could be counted upon to coöperate with the business and party elements. Jushin plans failed, however, when not a single eligible general would take the post of minister of war. Ugaki was forced to report that he could not form a cabinet. Again the army had exerted its power, and, unable to meet the challenge, the Jushin finally nominated General Hayashi Senjuro, a man acceptable to the army leaders. Hayashi took a stronger antiparty stand than had been taken by any premier up to this time. He insisted that members of his cabinet discard any party affiliations, and in his first statement of policy he called for the abandonment of party government. Actually, Hayashi's ideas were far more in line with the old "transcendental" concepts of the Meiji Genro than with the revolutionary concepts of the radical right or the ultranationalist concepts of most of the elements now dominating the army. The parties, however, naturally protested the Hayashi position, and the government was forced to dissolve the Diet only a few months after it came into power.

The resultant election of April, 1937, was the last competitive election in prewar Japan. The outcome was striking in only one respect: the Shakai Taishuto[1] captured 36 Diet seats (exactly double its number in 1936) and received more than 1,000,000 votes. Their could be no doubt that some of the urban classes

[1] The leftist Social Mass Party [ed.].

were turning to the Social Mass Party. However, the two major parties each polled more than three times the number of Shakai Taishuto votes, with the Minseito receiving 3,666,067 votes and 179 seats, and the Seiyukai receiving 3,608,882 votes and 174 seats. The military faced the same old problem that had plagued the early Meiji leaders. Without having their own party in the field, they could hardly win an election, and the elections of 1937 were considered a strong rebuke to Hayashi. Again, the electorate had leaned toward the moderates or progressives, and this time in even more decisive fashion, although absentee statistics were also higher.

Soon after the election, on June 3, 1937, the Hayashi cabinet resigned. The elder statesmen once more sought a candidate who would maintain in some fashion the balance of power between the army, the bureaucracy, and the parties, effecting such compromises as accorded with the requirements of the situation. This time, Konoe Fumimaro was finally persuaded to take the premiership. Konoe had long been a favorite of the army, but at the same time he had the general confidence of the Inner Court and of the party men. Konoe personalized the element of coöperation which existed among the conservative groups. In him were mirrored the confusions, the ambivalences, the drive for unity, the fear of radicalism, and the fatalism which were some of the ingredients of civilian capitulation and military power. And Konoe had been in office scarcely a month before the outbreak of the "Second China Incident." This was the beginning of Japan's last major crisis—one which expanded into global war and total defeat.

Even the façade of Japanese democracy was now doomed. It was only a question when and how the Diet and the old parties would be altered. Occasionally, the parties exercised their right of criticism vigorously enough to make trouble for some of the cabinets which followed that of Konoe. There were even a few outspoken individuals from party ranks who continued to defend effective parliamentary government. For the most part, however, the Diet members faithfully voted for government bills, maintained a discreet silence, and watched the growing international crisis with mixed hope and worry.

This crisis dealt the final blow to any efforts in the direction of restoring parliamentary rights and the prestige of the parties. The premium upon unity had never been greater. Now the military made concessions to the economic "pressure groups" in an effort to get maximum coöperation. Even without these concessions, however, the cleavages among the conservative groups which had shown up clearly in the 1936–1937 period would have diminished under the increasingly grave circumstances which Japan faced abroad. Complete harmony was never attained, but the war gave the military and their ideas additional priorities.

In their last few years, the old parties were torn apart by bitter factional struggles. Seiyukai factionalism became so intense that the party finally split into three sections after the resignation of Suzuki; the two most important fragments were led by Kuhara and Nakajima Chikuhei, another veteran politician. When the Nakajima forces took possession of Seiyukai headquarters and refused admittance to Kuhara's adherents, it provided momentary news interest to a press and public, which had become largely indifferent to party activities. The Minseito had internal problems of an almost equally serious nature, though it did not formally split up until just a few months before its complete dissolution. Even the Shakai Taishuto was deeply divided after 1937, and one strong group sought to unite with the nationalist parties. The members of the other group, led by Katayama Tetsu, remained faithful, for the most part, to the principles of social democracy, but they were prevented from organizing their projected *Kinro Kokuminto* (Workers' Nationalist Party), in May, 1940, by government edict.

Plans for a single new party had long been discussed in various circles. In some instances, these plans came from party men who saw in such a party the possibility of recouping political power or offering stronger opposition to authoritarianism. Increasingly, however, the idea of a new party focused on the theory of state unity and a controlled Diet. The most acceptable leader for a unity movement was Prince Konoe, and in the spring of 1940 he agreed to undertake the sponsorship of the new organization. Even before July 22, 1940, when his second cabinet was inaugurated, the old parties had begun to dissolve. The Shakai Taishuto went first, dissolving on July 3. The Kuhara faction of the Seiyukai followed, on July 16; the Kokumin Domei, on July 26; the Nakajima Seiyukai faction, on July 30; and, finally, the Minseito, on August 15. Various minor parties also went, and in slightly more than a month, the old parties had all left the political scene.

After the inevitable preliminary meetings, the *Taisei Yokusan Kai* (Imperial Rule Assistance Association) was inaugurated on October 12, 1940. The goal toward which many Japanese politicians of the past had striven now seemed to be realized. Japan had "one great party," dedicated to preserving internal unity, assisting the Emperor by formulating public opinion, and acting as a general propaganda outlet for the government. The new party was set up like a department, with various bureaus and with a detailed national organization. The opening sections from the regulations of the Provincial Planning Committee give some idea of its objectives and philosophy:

This association strives to establish a strong national defense structure by imbuing its members with the consciousness of being subjects of this empire; through mutual help and remonstrance taking the lead to become the propelling force of the people and always cooperating with the government as a medium for transmitting the wishes of the government as well as of the people at large.

We endeavor to be faithful loyal subjects. That is, we believe in our national structure, which is the manifestation of matchless absolute universal truth, faithfully observe the Imperial Rescripts of the successive sovereigns, serve the country in our respective posts, and exalt the great Divine Way.

The overwhelming majority of the old party leaders joined the Imperial Rule Assistance Association (IRRA), pledging themselves to work for its objectives. Actually, however, the "one great party" was not a spectacular success. The same old factionalisms, the same lack of mass appeal, the same problems of responsibility and leadership dogged its path. But parties based upon representative supremacy and a political competition were a thing of the past, and they had left a legacy of failure not easily to be forgotten.

. . . . In the period after 1931, the failure of the Japanese democratic movement was revealed in its entirety. Democratic philosophy and institutions were completely riddled by the sword thrusts of militarism and ultranationalism. But this was more an extension than a reversal of previous trends, and it was in accord with the predominant forces of modern Japanese society.

Japanese nationalism took most of its primary symbols from

a mixture of primitivism and Confucianism, both because these were central to Japanese tradition and because the agrarian-military class played the major role in the shaping and projection of the modern nationalist movement. The commercial-industrial forces were weak in numbers and social standing, but most important, it was not in the interest of these groups to attempt any basic reorientation of the nationalist themes. The prerequisites of their success and security seemed to lie in the same paternalism, "organic unity," and anti-individualism that had characterized the initial nationalist creed. To some of these concepts, indeed, they gave new significance, revealing the paradoxes implicit in nationalism from the standpoint of agrarian interests. Thus the struggle against centralized, capitalist domination accounted in large part for the early rural leadership of the democratic movement and for some agrarian sorties toward the "left." But the movement found its logical culmination in the "agrarian radicalism" of the period immediately after World War I. This radicalism was an attempt to bring tradition back to the side of agrarian supremacy; it was filled with ronin spirit, and the echoes of "Revere the Emperor—Oust the barbarian" rang out with resounding force. In its most central objective, of course, "agrarian radicalism" was defeated; it could not possibly succeed, since its major target was the industrial revolution. Yet it is not difficult to distinguish between the failure to attain its main objective and the success of its general themes, for in modified and extended form these themes had found general acceptance.

Moreover, they had been given additional potency by the techniques and ideas available to Japanese leadership after the Meiji Restoration. As has been noted, the drive for centralization in Japan was almost coincident with the full flowering of Western liberalism and its emphasis upon the common man. It was also practically coincident with the development of mass-media communications and education to reach that common man. The concept of leftist tutelage of the masses invariably emerged from these circumstances. But this was not necessarily an advantage for democracy. Indeed, as has been suggested, there were now new methods by which to avoid power sharing and additional reasons for so doing. Although the nature of modern Japanese society did not permit all these advanced techniques of mass control to be utilized, they were cultivated sufficiently through education and law to provide relative stability and canalize social unrest down a nationalist course. For nationalism in this setting could easily become the unifying force, the protector of elitist power, and the most logical compromise with the Western challenge.

These were the two great sources from which modern Japanese nationalism received its vitality, but there were a host of interrelated and additional factors which gave it tendency and power. Quite naturally, the measure of success in Japanese modernization, particularly the spectacular and unbroken chain of military victories (if one excepts Siberia), were important stimulants. The victory over Russia in 1904–1905 became the great nationalist symbol. It was used for the purpose of expounding such varied themes as the superiority of spirit over resources, the perfidy of the West, the importance of absolute unity, and the duty to keep faith with those who had sacrificed themselves for the cause of the nation. In terms of military exploits abroad, there was little to destroy the myth of Japanese invincibility and superiority.

If one probes deeply, however, he discovers that the elements of doubt, conflict, and crisis in modern Japan were at least as important as those of success in influencing the nationalist movement. Despite superficial signs to the contrary, modern Japan was a society filled with fundamental conflicts and hence driven to push nationalism ever further in an effort to attain some greater measure of internal unity and to combat the divisive forces effectively. The scope of these conflicts was so broad as to defy description, but fundamentally almost all of them were connected with the problem of assimilating the industrial phase of Western evolution. They were intensified, moreover, by the extraordinary speed and particular timing which marked the process of assimilation, by the contradictory and transitional nature of the West itself, and by the growing world crisis which enveloped the twentieth century.

A virulent nationalism was a most natural product of these conditions. It was not only an attack upon the problems of the rising rural-urban cleavage and growing sense of class divisions; it was a counterattack against Western imperialism, discrimination, and attitudes of superiority or indifference. It was a psychological weapon against the corrosive tendencies of doubt, confusion, and an inferiority complex in a people under the greatest emotional tension. And given the nature of the contemporary world, it was an inevitable by-product of the profound economic and political problems which modernization had bequeathed to Japanese society. Nor was it unique. Its pendulum-like swing closely followed world tendencies, and both its causes and its results had striking parallels in such Western societies as that of Germany.

Thus Japanese nationalism reached its culmination in the 1930's and became the driving force in that era which has often been labeled "Military-Fascist." It is clear that there were some important differences between this Japanese "Fascism" and its Western counterpart. In the first place, the concept of *der Führer* was absent in Japan. There was a great difference between a Hitler and a Tojo, and this reflected the complete lack of individualism in Japanese society. Moreover, Japanese "Fascism," as was noted earlier, never approached a mass movement. Those national socialist elements dedicated to this end failed, just as they failed to effect a *coup d'état* in the fashion of the march on Rome. Here again, certain basic elements of modern Japan were revealed, for given the nature of that society, the difficulties of creating a mass movement were substantial. The failure of the "radical right" allowed a great measure of traditional elitism to dominate in the Japanese militarist era, and partially because of this, that era was never as completely authoritarian as the Nazi regime.

Yet, were these differences fundamental when compared with the similarities? In both cases, Fascism was a basic attack upon individualism, democracy, Marxism and internationalism. It was profoundly anti-intellectual, emphasizing the myth, the hero, and action. It forwarded irrationalism to new heights. It found its foremost expressions in a glorification of war and of the racial spirit. Many of its roots were agrarian, and among its most primary supporters were elements of the rural classes. Thus it reflected within it much of the primitivism implanted in a pre-industrial society. It built up its own *raison d'être* through an ever expanding campaign of foreign aggression, meanwhile retreating from its initial anti-capitalist position. Finally, the intensive emphasis of Fascism upon cultural uniqueness could not hide the fact that it was a common development among societies with widely different "cultural heritages" but with similar modern problems of timing and development.

23 FROM   *Kita Ikki*
Plan for the Reorganization of Japan, 1919

*Populist and agrarian anticapitalism, nationalism, and the re-
jection of liberalism and democracy characterized many of the
proposals for a "New Restoration" of Imperial power in the
Japan of the 1920s. Perhaps the most important of these proposals
was the one formulated by Kita Ikki in 1919, selections from
which are reprinted here.*

At present the Japanese empire is faced with a national crisis
unparalleled in its history; it faces dilemmas at home and
abroad. The vast majority of the people feel insecure in their
livelihood and they are on the point of taking a lesson from the
collapse of European societies, while those who monopolize political, military, and economic power simply hide themselves and,
quaking with fear, try to maintain their unjust position. Abroad,
neither England, America, Germany, nor Russia has kept its
word, and even our neighbor China, which long benefited from
the protection we provided through the Russo-Japanese War, not
only has failed to repay us but instead despises us. Truly we are
a small island, completely isolated in the Eastern Sea. One false
step and our nation will again fall into the desperate state of
crisis—dilemmas at home and abroad—that marked the period
before and after the Meiji Restoration.

The only thing that brightens the picture is the sixty million
fellow countrymen with whom we are blessed. The Japanese
people must develop a profound awareness of the great cause of
national existence and of the people's equal rights, and they
need an unerring, discriminating grasp of the complexities of
domestic and foreign thought. The Great War in Europe was,
like Noah's flood, Heaven's punishment on them for arrogant

SOURCE. Ryusaku Tsunoda, William Theodore de Bary, Donald Keene,
compilers, *Sources of Japanese Tradition*, Vol. II, pp. 268–277. (New York:
Columbia University Press, 1958.) Reprinted by permission of Columbia University Press.

and rebellious ways. It is of course natural that we cannot look to the Europeans, who are out of their minds because of the great destruction, for a completely detailed set of plans. But in contrast Japan, during those five years of destruction, was blessed with five years of fulfillment. Europe needs to talk about reconstruction, while Japan must move on to reorganization. The entire Japanese people, thinking calmly from this perspective which is the result of Heaven's rewards and punishments, should, in planning how the great Japanese empire should be reorganized, petition for a manifestation of the imperial prerogative establishing "a national opinion in which no dissenting voice is heard, by the organization of a great union of the Japanese people." Thus, by homage to the emperor, a basis for national reorganization can be set up.

Truly, our seven hundred million brothers in China and India have no path to independence other than that offered by our guidance and protection. And for our Japan, whose population has doubled within the past fifty years, great areas adequate to support a population of at least two hundred and forty or fifty millions will be absolutely necessary a hundred years from now. For a nation, one hundred years are like a hundred days for an individual. How can those who are anxious about these inevitable developments, or who grieve over the desperate conditions of neighboring countries, find their solace in the effeminate pacifism of doctrinaire socialism? I do not necessarily rule out social progress by means of the class struggle. But still, just what kind of so-called science is it that can close its eyes to the competition between peoples and nations which has taken place throughout the entire history of mankind? At a time when the authorities in the European and American revolutionary creeds have found it completely impossible to arrive at an understanding of the "gospel of the sword" because of their superficial philosophy, the noble Greece of Asian culture must complete her national reorganization on the basis of her own national polity. At the same time, let her lift the virtuous banner of an Asian league and take the leadership in a world federation which must come. In so doing let her proclaim to the world the Way of Heaven in which all are children of Buddha, and let her set the example which the world must follow. So the ideas of people like those who oppose arming the nation are after all simply childish.

SECTION ONE: THE PEOPLE'S EMPEROR

Suspension of the Constitution. In order for the emperor and the entire Japanese people to establish a secure base for the national reorganization, the emperor will, by a show of his imperial prerogative, suspend the Constitution for a period of three years, dissolve both houses of the Diet, and place the entire nation under martial law. . . .

(Note 2: Those who look upon a *coup d'état* as an abuse of power on behalf of a conservative autocracy ignore history. Napoleon's *coup d'état* in refusing to cooperate with reactionary elements offered the only out for the Revolution at a time when the parliament and the press were alive with royalist elements. And even though one sees in the Russian Revolution an incident in which Lenin dissolved with machine guns a parliament filled with obstructionists, the popular view is still that a *coup d'état* is a reactionary act.)

(Note 3: A *coup d'état* should be looked upon as a direct manifestation of the authority of the nation; that is, of the will of society. The progressive leaders have all arisen from popular groups. They arise because of political leaders like Napoleon and Lenin. In the reorganization of Japan there must be a manifestation of the power inherent in a coalition of the people and sovereign.)

(Note 4: The reason why the Diet must be dissolved is that the nobility and the wealthy upon whom it depends are incapable of standing with the emperor and the people in the cause of reorganization. The necessity for suspension of the Constitution is that these people seek protection in the law codes enacted under it. The reason martial law must be proclaimed is that it is essential for the freedom of the nation that there be no restraint in suppressing the opposition which will come from the above groups.

However, it will also be necessary to suppress those who propagate a senseless and half-understood translation of outside revolutionary creeds as the agents of reorganization.)

The True Significance of the Emperor. The fundamental doctrine of the emperor as representative of the people and as pillar of the nation must be made clear.

In order to clarify this a sweeping reform of the imperial court in the spirit of the Emperor Jimmu in founding the state and in the spirit of the great Meiji emperor will be carried out. The present Privy Councillors and other officials will be dismissed from their posts, and in their place will come talent, sought throughout the realm, capable of assisting the emperor.

A Consultative Council (*Kōmonin*) will be established to assist the emperor. Its members, fifty in number, will be appointed by the emperor.

A member of the Consultative Council must tender his resignation to the emperor whenever the cabinet takes action against him or whenever the Diet passes a vote of nonconfidence against him. However, the Council members are by no means responsible to either the cabinet or to the Diet. . . .

(Note 2: There is no scientific basis whatever for the belief of the democracies that a state which is governed by representatives voted in by the electorate is superior to a state which has a system of government by a particular person. Every nation has its own national spirit and history. It cannot be maintained, as advocates of this theory would have it, that China during the first eight years of the republic was more rational than Belgium, which retained rule by a single person. The "democracy" of the Americans derives from the very unsophisticated theory of the time which held that society came into being through a voluntary contract based upon the free will of individuals; these people, emigrating from each European country as individuals, established communities and built a country. But their theory of the divine right of voters is a half-witted philosophy which arose in opposition to the theory of the divine right of kings at that time. Now Japan certainly was not founded in this way, and there has never been a period in which Japan was dominated by a half-witted philosophy. Suffice it to say that the system whereby the head of state has to struggle for election by a long-winded self-advertisement and by exposing himself to ridicule like a low-class actor seems a very strange custom to the Japanese people, who have been brought up in the belief that silence is golden and that modesty is a virtue.) . . . .

The Abolition of the Peerage System. The peerage system will be abolished, and the spirit of the Meiji Restoration will be clarified by removal of this barrier which has come between the emperor and the people.

The House of Peers will be abolished and replaced by a Council of Deliberation (*Shingiin*), which shall consider action taken by the House of Representatives.

The Council of Deliberation will be empowered to reject decisions taken by the House of Representatives a single time. The members of the Council of Deliberation will consist of distinguished men in many fields of activity, elected by each other and appointed by the emperor. . . .

Universal Suffrage. All men twenty-five years of age, by their rights as people of Great Japan, will have the right, freely and equally, to stand for election to and to vote for the House of Representatives. The same will hold for local self-government assemblies.

Women will not have the right to participate in politics. . . .

The Restoration of the People's Freedom. The various laws which have restricted the freedom of the people and impaired the spirit of the constitution in the past—the Civil Service Appointment Ordinance, the Peace Preservation police law, the Press Act, the Publication Law, and similar measures—will be abolished.

(Note: This is obviously right. These laws work only to maintain all sorts of cliques.)

The National Reorganization Cabinet. A Reorganization Cabinet will be organized while martial law is in effect; in addition to the present ministries, it will have ministries for industries and several Ministers of State without Portfolio. Members of the Reorganization Cabinet will not be chosen from the present military, bureaucratic, financial, and party cliques, but this task will be given to outstanding individuals selected throughout the whole country. . . .

The National Reorganization Diet. The National Reorganization Diet, elected in a general election and convened during the period of martial law, will deliberate on measures for reorganization.

The National Reorganization Diet will not have the right to deliberate on the basic policy of national reorganization proclaimed by the emperor.

(Note 1: Since in this way the people will become the main force and the emperor the commander, this *coup d'état* will not be an abuse of power but the expression of the national determination by the emperor and the people.) . . . .

(Note 3: If a general election were to be held in our present society of omnipotent capital and absolutist bureaucracy the majority of the men elected to the Diet would either be opposed to the reorganization or would receive their election expenses from men opposed to the reorganization. But, since the general election will be held and the Diet convened under martial law, it will of course be possible to curb the rights of harmful candidates and representatives.) . . . .

24 FROM *General Araki*
On the Spirit and Destiny of Japan

A second important strain in the growth of "fascism from below" was the militarism and imperialism of the so-called "Imperial Way Faction" in the Army high command. General Araki played an important role in this faction, serving in the Inukai and Saito cabinets (1932–1934) and actively supporting the Japanese invasion of Manchuria (the so-called "Manchurian Incident") of 1931. Following is a selection from his memorial on The Spirit and Destiny of Japan.

THOUGHTS ON THE SPIRIT OF JAPAN

The secret of victory in war is knowledge of oneself and one's adversary. This is a basic principle which applies to everything. Without knowing oneself, one can know nothing.

I think that for Japan to get out of the present difficult situation there is no other means than that the entire Japanese people decidedly and fully realize they are Japanese. Only then will the development of Japan get its full swing when this self-realization is achieved.

SOURCE. Araki Sadao, "The Spirit and Destiny of Japan," English translation printed in O. Tanin and E. Yohan, *Militarism and Fascism in Japan*, pp. 301–304. (New York: International Publishers, 1934). Reprinted by permission of International Publishers.

But what must be the concrete object of such self-realization by the Japanese? What is the fundamental distinguishing trait of Japan? This is nothing but the great ideal, represented by the three regalias of the Japanese dynasty: Jasper, a mirror and a sword which were the presents of Amaterasuomikami at the creation of the Japanese state. As every Japanese knows these three regalias are the symbols:

> the mirror—of justice
> the jasper—of mercy
> the sword—of bravery

It is justice, mercy and bravery, represented by the regalias of the Japanese dynasty that are the fundamental ideals of the Japanese state, the way marked out by the Emperors. This is the so-called real "Imperial Course." Japanese history represents nothing but the realization of this course. To preserve this course, make it a glorious one, is the duty of the Japanese people as loyal subjects of His Majesty.

The fundamental essence of the Japanese system of government is the unity of high and low; of the Monarch and his people. This points clearly to the aim of the Japanese, which amounts to the glorification of the Emperor, for which purpose public welfare must take precedence over private, personal welfare.

And then, when the Japanese people will master this genuinely national spirit and realize its true purpose, it will naturally follow that it will strengthen its own development.

The present difficult situation cannot be overcome until the Japanese people will be inspired with the desire to realize with maximum determination its great ideal of world significance. Without this inspiration it is impossible either to solve the Manchuro-Mongolian problem or that of continental policy.

All this is confirmed by such historical facts as took place beginning with the Meiji Era, like the Japanese-Chinese, the Japano-Russian and the Japano-German wars, solemnly conducted under this great ideal. Japan's position was then acknowledged by the whole world. On this basis arose the greatness of the Japanese state and its power grew and strengthened. If these wars had been conducted by Japan on the basis of egoistic interest, if they had been of a predatory plundering character, then Japan would in all probability have been the subject of reproach on the part of all the governments of the world and would finally have found itself in a difficult position, bordering on an impasse. Germany during the recent European war was a living example of this.

From the very beginning of history Japanese superiority consisted in this, that evil and injustice never guided its actions, never took the place of high virtue in its deeds.

Now there is, however, a basis for disquietude, as there are groups among the people, though few in number, but who taken in by foreign radical ideology and following Marxian theories sometimes forget the honor of Japan, its aims and their duty. There are also people that are conducting themselves in a way which leads to ruin, as they give themselves over to slothfulness and rest while lacking ideals and consciousness.

It is unnecessary to speak here of the fact that the theory of materialism that does not recognize the spiritual functions of man, transforming him into a machine, robbing him of his ideals and freedom, transforming him into a public slave—is harmful for a healthy society.

We, who believe in Japanese traditions and the Japanese spirit, strongly desire that the entire Japanese people quickly awake from their evil sleep and, united under the great ideal, become the preacher-apostle of high Imperial virtue.

JAPAN AND PEACE

Now let us consider the external position of Japan.

Since Japan, beginning with the Meiji Era, has shown the whole world its real, sincere face, it has always acted on the basis of justice and had the determination to resort to real force, sacrificing itself for the benefit of the world. It never hesitated in the matter of the annihilation of evil. As a result it has become one of the three greatest powers of the world.

To give support to the greatness of the Emperor means to realize the great ideal of Great Japan. For this purpose the Japanese people gathered all its forces as it burned with the great self-realization as the Japanese people.

However, lately, this strong national enthusiasm is gradually waning, it can even be said it is in a severely fallen state.

As an example, we shall take the spread of frivolous ideology in society. Capitalists are concerned only with their own interests and pay no attention to public life; politicians often forget the general situation in the country while absorbed in their party interests; clerks and students forget their duty giving themselves over to merriment and pleasures.

In a word, it can be said that there is frivolity everywhere, egoism replacing cheerfulness, honor and ideals. Who can fail to be disquieted about the future of the state when thinking over the further results of such a situation? And this is not only a question of the future. Signs of disaster are already adumbrated.

In reality we have the important sad fact of the isolation of Japan in its international position—and the Japanese people must know that until they will not abandon their indifference, Japan will always be subject to such a position of isolation.

It is necessary to study the causes of this without delay. They consist in this—that the Japanese have forgotten their national self-realization, forgotten the correct understanding of Imperial Japan.

What can remain of Japan when the great soul of the state is forgotten, when national pride is abandoned? The fact that Japan is now an object of disdain on the part of the entire world and has been insulted by China is in the long run the fault of Japan itself. It must be well understood that this is the origin of the Manchurian incident as well as the attack on Japan on the part of the governments united in the League of Nations.

I repeat, the present Manchurian incident arose not on the basis of such trivial questions as the ignoring of treaty obligations or the infringement of the rights and interests of Japan. The fundamental reason for the incident is the insult of Japan by China. The League of Nations could not distinguish between justice and injustice which brought about the result that it too insults Japan. It must thus be evident to everybody that the direct cause of Japanese isolation lies in the insult received by it from all the world and that this happened by the fault of Japan itself.

The Japanese people must understand this clearly. It must also understand that only by mastering this truth can it get out of the present difficulties.

In the face of such a situation the Manchurian incident is for

Japan a sign of God. It must be admitted that God has given the alarm in order to awaken the Japanese people.

We are by no means pessimistic with regard to the present difficult situation. We firmly believe that the present international situation will rapidly improve for Japan if the Japanese people will be regenerated with the great soul of the Japanese state and show itself as the Japanese people. On this condition the time will soon come when the entire world will joyously welcome Imperial virtue.

25   FROM   *Masao Maruyama*
From "Fascism from Below" to "Fascism from Above"

Professor Maruyama, an eminent Japanese political scientist and a Marxist, divides the development of Japanese fascism into three stages: the "preparatory period," from 1919 to the "Manchurian Incident" of 1931, a "period of right-wing movements among civilians"; the "period of maturity," from 1931 to the "February Incident" of 1936, during which "the military became the driving force of the fascist movement"; and the "consummation period," from 1936 till the defeat of Japan on 15 August 1945, during which "the military, now the open supporters of fascism from above, fashioned an unstable ruling structure in coalition with the semi-feudal power of the bureaucracy and the Senior Retainers on the one hand, and with monopoly capital and the political parties on the other" (pages 26–27). The following section deals with the transition from "fascism from below" to "fascism from above." (It is worth bearing in mind, when one notices the decisive role played by the army, that imperialist military aggression was not an end product of fascism in Japan—as it was in Italy and Germany—but a concomitant of its de-

SOURCE. Masao Maruyama, *Thought and Behaviour in Modern Japanese Politics*, edited by Ivan Morris, pp. 65–74. (London: Oxford University Press, 1963). Reprinted by permission of Oxford University Press.

*velopment and, perhaps, a decisive factor in its triumph, since
it gave the army a weight in political affairs it might otherwise
not have had.)*

The distinctive characteristic in the development of Japanese
fascism, was, as we have seen, that it never took the form of a
fascist revolution with a mass organization occupying the State
apparatus from outside the administration. The process was
rather the gradual maturing of a fascist structure within the
State, effected by the established political forces of the military,
the bureaucracy, and the political parties.

Yet it should not be suggested that the activities of the civilian
right-wing movement and of the revolutionary young officers
were therefore of no great historical significance. The trend towards fascism in the lower strata of society and the spasmodic
outbursts of the radical fascist movement were a continual stimulus to the advance of fascism from above. The important point
is that the fascization of the ruling structure developed step by
step, with the military and the bureaucracy as its axis and with
the social energy of this radical fascism as its springboard. For
example, the October Incident took place immediately after the
Manchurian Incident; at about the same time the movement
towards fascism from within the established political parties also
became marked in the movement of the Home Minister, Mr.
Adachi, for a coalition Cabinet.

The May 15 Incident put an end to the short history of politi-
cal party government in Japan. A coalition of the military, the
bureaucracy, and the political parties first emerged in the Saitō
Cabinet (May 1932). Again, the right of the military to a voice
in politics was advanced a step further after the Heaven-Sent
Soldiers' Unit Incident. On the occasion of the Grand Army
Manoeuvres in Kyūshū in November 1933 the Joint Council for
Rural Policy was organized by the Agriculture Minister, Mr.
Gotō Fumio, the War Minister, General Araki, and key officers
of the General Staff; and it was from that time that the military
as a whole began to take a more positive interest in the question
of the villages.

The reform movement of the young officers extends like an unbroken chain from the Officers' School Incident through the Aizawa Incident and on to the February Incident. Regardless of the intentions of the participants, each of these incidents expanded the political domain of the top section of the military. The February Incident above all proved to be a turning-point. This was of course the final and biggest of the successive fascist *putsches*. Thereafter the fascist movement from below, led by young officers or the civilian radical right wing, retires into the background.

As the Army purge got under way, the Imperial Way Faction was overwhelmed at a single stroke by the Control Faction, or rather, by an anti-Imperial Way Faction coalition. Hegemony was taken from Araki, Mazaki, Yanagawa, and Obata, and grasped by Umezu, Tōjō, Sugiyama, and Koiso.

The powers forming this new direction group thereafter carried out a thorough purge within the Army. While suppressing the influence of radical fascism, they successively realized the political demands of the military, using the menace of radical fascism as a decoy for outsiders. When General Terauchi joined the Hirota Cabinet just after the February Incident, he imposed conditions from the outset, refusing admittance to the Cabinet of persons he regarded as tinged with liberalism. On his appointment as War Minister, Terauchi issued a frankly fascist declaration for "the renovation of general administration; the renunciation of liberalism; the establishment of a totalitarian system." He presented political demands that would limit the franchise through a revised electoral law and that would maim the Diet by abolishing control of the legislature over the executive. While suppressing fascism from below, then, this fascism from above made rapid progress. The fate of Kita, Nishida, and the young officers of the February Incident is justly expressed in the Chinese proverb, "when the cunning hares have been killed, the hunting dogs go into the cooking pot."

The circumstances of this period may also be understood by comparing the punishments awarded after the May 15 Incident with those of the February Incident. The military defendants of the May 15 Incident all received light punishments. Gotō and the ten other military defendants were sentenced to four years' imprisonment; all were subsequently pardoned and discharged from prison in 1936. In the case of the Navy defendants, Koga Scishi and Mikami Taku as the ringleaders received the heaviest sentences of fifteen years' imprisonment; of the others, one was sentenced to thirteen years, three to ten years, one to two years, and one to one year of imprisonment. By 1940 all had been pardoned and set free. These were the punishments for an incident in which armed groups burst into the official residence of the Premier in broad daylight, assassinating him and terrorizing the capital. Yet the War Minister, General Araki, in a public statement just after the May 15 Incident, declared:

"We cannot restrain our tears when we consider the mentality expressed in the actions of these pure and naïve young men. They are not actions for fame, or personal gain, nor are they traitorous. They were performed in the sincere belief that they were for the benefit of Imperial Japan. Therefore, in dealing with this incident, it will not do to dispose of it in a routine manner according to shortsighted conceptions."

The Navy Minister, Admiral Ōsumi, stated: "When one considers what caused these pure-hearted young men to make this mistake, it demands the most serious reflection."

One can understand, then, how much the military as a whole was in sympathy with this incident. In contrast, Kōda Kiyosada and sixteen other military ringleaders of the February Incident were all executed. And by a judgement some months after the February Incident Lieutenant-Colonel Aizawa was sentenced to death for his assassination of Nagata, the Director of the Military Affairs Bureau, in a previous incident in which he alone had been implicated.

These cases are sufficient to indicate the sudden change in the attitude of the military towards incidents of this kind. At a special conference after the February 26 Incident the War Minister, General Terauchi, made the following statement:

"If we put together the declaration of their motives for rising and their reported statements, it appears that the motive behind this incident was an attempt to clarify the national polity and to carry out a so-called Shōwa Restoration. We admit that in the present state of the country, which has driven them to act in this way, there are many matters requiring correction and renovation.

We are, however, unfortunately obliged to note that at the root of their guiding principle there lies an idea of national reformation which is harboured by a group of extremists outside the Army and which is totally contrary to our national polity."

By "an idea of national reformation harboured by a group outside the Army," Terauchi is presumably referring to the ideas of Kita Ikki. In any case his categorical condemnation of the uprising as an act incompatible with the national polity reveals the extent of the sudden change in the attitude of the military leaders since the May 15 Incident. The "New Control Faction," which grasped hegemony after the February Incident, included many officers who as members of the Cherry Blossom Association had stood for reform by *coup d'état*. Now that they were in power, however, they declared an Army purge, rejecting the participation of military men in politics except through the War Minister and suppressing radical tendencies.

Just after the war the Imperial Way Faction maintained that it had been largely opposed to Tōjō. But the struggle between the Imperial Way and Control Factions was not simply one between those who stood for a principle and those who resorted to conspiratorial devices. It had much more the character of a struggle between factions and cliques. The February Incident merely gave the New Control Faction the opportunity to suppress the Imperial Way Faction linked with the radical young officers and to establish their own hegemony. According to Terauchi, the February Incident was an action contrary to the national polity. But, according to the young officers, "The reconstruction plan [Kita's plan for the reconstruction of Japan] is in complete accord with the national polity. Indeed, it is the manifestation of the national polity as a State organization and as an economic system." In their opinion, the members of the Control Faction, while repeating the word "national polity," were constantly trying to exploit the authority of the Emperor in order to carry out their own political ideology. According to the furious denunciations of the young officers, it was Staff members of the Control Faction who did not hesitate to come forth with statements like: "If the Emperor does not agree, we will make him listen at the point of a dagger."

This is an extremely interesting point: the actions of the Im-

perial Way Faction, such as mobilizing troops and starting uprisings, were apparently very radical. But the content of their
ideology was extremely vague and abstract, being the principle
of accepting the absolute authority of the Emperor and sub-
mitting humbly to his wishes. One of the reasons that the participants' plans covered only the violent stage of the operation
and were not concerned with the aftermath is that their thoughts
were based on the principle of the absolute authority of the
Emperor. In other words, any attempt at formulating plans of
reconstruction would be tantamount to surmising the will of the
Emperor and thus an invasion of the Imperial prerogative. This
leads to a mythological sort of optimism according to which, if
only evil men could be removed from the Court, if only the
dark clouds shrouding the Emperor could be swept away, the
Imperial sun would naturally shine forth.

In comparison, the men of the Control Faction may be regarded as more rational, and they may be blamed for consciously
using the Emperor in order to realize their own plan from above.
As a result the political process after the February Incident was
the "rationalization" of Japanese fascism, which ceased to take
the form of radical uprisings but advanced steadily by legal
means from within the governmental apparatus. During the sev-
entieth session of the Diet (1936–7) Mr. Hamada Kunimatsu put
a question to the War Minister, General Terauchi, which incidentally provoked the so-called hara-kiri exchange between them.
In the course of this question he stated: "We cannot suppress
our regret at the appearance of a new political evil: as the Army
purge progresses, the reformed Army is strongly asserting itself
as a driving force in politics." This was a keen verbal thrust at
the paradoxical effect of the Army purge.

Soon after the suppression of radical fascism, a closer alliance
of the military, the bureaucracy, and the zaibatsu was consolidated
and an advance was made towards a "completed" form of fascism. In the financial policy of Baba in the Hirota Cabinet the
slogan was "national defence in the widest sense." It was against
the background of the troubled social atmosphere after the February Incident that such a slogan was raised; and the budget for
unemployment grants and agrarian relief was coupled with increased military expenditure. This extremely inflationary policy
gave rise to great apprehension in financial circles. So in the

Yūki economic policy, which succeeded it and which was backed by financial interests, a reversal was made to "national defence in the narrow sense" of military expenditure alone. The grants in Baba's policy for the financial regeneration of the villages were all cut down and grants for local government finance were cancelled. At this time Mr. Yūki came out with the famous words: "Henceforth I wish to proceed in close embrace with the military," and the term "close-embrace finance" arose from this.

As an example of this state of affairs, we may note the memorial drawn up by the standing committee of the Japan Economic League on 3 March 1937:

"Recent internal and external conditions make increased national expenditure centred upon military expenditure unavoidable. But an over-rapid expansion of government finance would lead to an insufficiency in domestic productive power and to a rise in prices. There is no way to avoid this contradiction except by restricting government expenditure to necessary and indispensable items. Therefore any increase in administrative expenditure apart from military expenditure should be restricted as far as possible, and at the same time the budget should be drawn up for the next three years on the policy of giving priority to national defence expenditure."

This is representative of opinion in business circles at that time. Thus the interests of business groups and the military drew nearer, and a "close-embrace" structure of Japanese fascism came to completion.

The fascist movement from below was completely absorbed into totalitarian transformation from above. Thereafter, as the international situation intensified for Japan on the outbreak of the China Incident, the "unity of the entire nation" became an absolute demand. In the name of national polity a triangular formation was established consisting of the bureaucracy, which had no footing among the people, the military, which called itself the driving force of reformation but which would never assume any political responsibility, and the political parties, which were constantly wrangling and yet had already lost their fighting spirit for a struggle against fascism. Between the Hirota and the Tōjō Cabinets, the Hayashi, first Konoe, Hiranuma, Abe, Yonai, second Konoe, and third Konoe Cabinets were organized in quick succession. Every change in the balance of power between the three powers resulted in a Cabinet change. There arose here the freak phenomenon that the more a 'strong Cabinet' became the watchword, the harder it was to find a nucleus in government.

But this does not imply any slackening in the move towards fascism. It should not be forgotten that in this period important steps were taken one after another in the direction of outright fascism. In late 1937 and early 1938 there was the general round-up of professors close to the Labour-Peasant Faction, the leaders of the National Council of Trade Unions, and those of the Japan Proletariat Party. Also in 1938 there was the ordinance for the permanent prohibition of May Day and the promulgation of the National General Mobilization Law. In March 1939 Japan withdrew from international labour organizations. In 1940 there occurred the dissolution of all the political parties, beginning with the Social Masses Party, the dissolution of the Japan Federation of Labour, the inauguration of the Imperial Rule Assistance Association and of the Great Japan Serve-the-State-through-Industry Association, and the conclusion of the Tripartite Pact. Rome was not built in a day, and the Tōjō dictatorship did not come into existence all of a sudden.

Konoe's New Order Movement throws valuable light on these developments. It aimed at strengthening political leadership by organizing the people, and sprang from an awareness that the existing political instability was due to the lack of a popular foundation. The motivation of the New Order Movement is extremely complex and cannot be described in a few words, but this was at any rate its original intention. However, the movement ran up against the stumbling-block of the absolute Emperor system, and was suspected by the national polity faction of being a kind of Shogunate. As a result it became an emasculated and formalized bureaucratic organ. This was the so-called "transformation" of the Assistance Association from a political to a moral movement. At the outset it was said that the Association was designed to "transmit the will of the authorities to the people, and to articulate the will of the people to the authorities." Soon, however, the expression, "the will of the people," was being criticized as being contrary to the national polity, and it was revised to read, "making the conditions of the people known to the authorities." This should suffice to show how much even the faintest tinge of popular initiative was disliked.

In January 1942, as a supplement to the formalized Assistance Association, the Imperial Rule Assistance Young Men's Corps was set up, but this too was not a political society. Since its basic aim was to act as a subordinate organization of the Assistance Association, it was incapable of vigorous activity. In some districts troublesome issues arose between the Assistance Association and the Young Men's Corps. In April 1942 the so-called Assistance election was carried out, and in the May of that year the Imperial Rule Assistance Political Association was formed as the sole political association in existence. But this was a conglomeration of existing political influences of all kinds, in which radical fascist groups, members of the previous political parties, right-wing idealists, and converted members of the proletarian parties were all gathered together. As a result it became completely vacuous as a political movement.

These meanderings trace the course of the efforts that were made to build the political structure of Japan on the organized masses as in Germany and Italy. But all such movements ended in complete absorption within the bureaucratic hierarchy. Japanese fascism was never able to achieve a firmly organized popular foundation. The Central Co-operative Assembly, set up in conjunction with the Assistance Movement, was a purely advisory organ simply for "making the conditions of the people known to the authorities." The drafts of proposals expressed within it had no legal binding power. The government merely "noted" them. At the time, the Assistance Association brought out a pamphlet entitled "About the Co-operative Assembly" in which the following statement is made:

"The various questions presented to this Assembly will be heard by the government and by the Assistance Association, and will be promptly adopted or rejected after serious consideration. The important thing is to handle government policy with the sweet and harmonious co-operation that prevails in a family. . . . In short, we think that this Council, in being adaptable and unobstructive, extra-legislative and without legal functions, is of great political value. Its fragile constitution seems at first sight to be its weak point, but it is precisely this fragility that gives it its charm."

This is an apt illustration of the way in which the authorities thought during this period.

Finally, with the outbreak of the Pacific War, we come to the Tōjō dictatorship. Neither the Imperial Way Faction nor the Control Faction any longer existed. All influences troublesome to Tōjō were singled out and all opposition groups suppressed by new measures such as the Law for the Emergency Control of Speech, Publication, Meeting, and Association, and the Special Law for Wartime Crimes. Even the right-wing groups, who prided themselves on their traditions, were forcibly dissolved into the Assistance Association and the Asia Development League. Tōjō himself, being Premier, War Minister, War Supplies Minister, and Chief of Staff, wielded unprecedented authority. Now for the first time a strong dictatorial government approaching that of Hitler and Mussolini seemed to emerge.

But the foundation of its strength lay chiefly in the military police net spread out over the whole country. Japanese fascism never possessed a distinctive popular organization like those in Germany and Italy. It met the catastrophe of 15 August 1945 with the bureaucratic leadership and the sham constitutionalism of the Meiji era still intact.

26 FROM *Prince Fumimaro Konoe*
On the New Order Movement

August 1937 saw the beginning of the "China Incident"—the Japanese invasion of China. In October 1938 the Prime Minister, Prince Konoe, announced the establishment of a New Order in East Asia (later called the Greater East Asia Co-Prosperity Sphere). In August 1940 Prince Konoe, Prime Minister once again, and

SOURCE. *The Japan Year Book* (The Foreign Affairs Association of Japan, Tokyo, 1941) pp. 165–177: Prince Konoe's Statement. Reprinted by permission of The Foreign Affairs Association of Japan.

with a mandate to organize Japan along totalitarian lines, disclosed the nature and purpose of the New Order Movement. It confirms the view that fascism adopts forms suited to the society in which it arises, but has as its essence everywhere the suppression of opposition, the enlistment of the nation's resources—material and human—in the great "Cause," and the creation of a predatory warfare society that is to bypass, by means of aggression abroad, the social, economic and political problems that exist at home, and which it fails or refuses to solve by either revolution or reform.

"In the midst of a world-wide disturbance, Japan is now going forward with an unparalleled task, the creation of a new order in East Asia. If Japan is to bring the China Affair to a successful conclusion, while adjusting herself to the international situation, and to take an active part in the establishment of a new world order, she must concentrate on this task the total power of the nation to the utmost degree so as to be in a position to take in an independent manner, swiftly and resolutely, appropriate measures for meeting whatever situation may arise.

"To this end Japan must perfect a national defense structure of the highest degree. The basis of such a structure is a powerful internal structure. Consequently there has arisen the pressing demand for the establishment of a new structure in politics, economy, education, culture and all the domains of the life of the State and of the people.

"This indeed is a national demand, transcending a Cabinet, a faction or an individual. It is not a demand of a temporary character for carrying out any specific policy, but of a permanent one, for rendering possible the powerful pursuance of any policy, when the necessity arises. Whether or not Japan can establish such a strong national structure will decide the very rise or fall of the nation.

"Among the items to be considered in this new organization of the nation must be mentioned the harmonious cooperation between the High Command and the administrative branch of the Government, the consolidation of State mechanisms and the heightening of efficiency, and the establishment of a new parliamentary structure as an organ for assisting the Throne. The Government, on their part, are exerting utmost efforts in order to achieve these ends. But of far greater importance is the first establishment of that "national structure" which is to serve as the very foundation of all and under which the people are to fulfil effectively their duty of assisting the Throne.

"The aim of the new national structure is to unite the total energies of the State and of the people, to make one living whole of our hundred million fellow countrymen and enable them all to fulfil perfectly their duty as subjects of the Throne. To attain this goal, each one of us must be enabled to fulfil that duty in the performance of his daily task. It is but natural that when the majority of the people, as it has been the case in the past, have no opportunity to take part in government other than when they are called to cast a vote once every three or four years, they would not as a whole take to heart the destiny of the country.

"The organization of the nation is that which enables the people to serve the nation in their everyday life: it must therefore extend to the economic and cultural spheres. There must be a solid nationwide structure in which all component parts are organized vertically, and they are also bound together horizontally. It is because there does not exist such a structure allowing the people to assist effectively the Throne that we see today a tendency toward a conflict between those who govern and those who are governed, a lack of true understanding on the part of the authorities who formulate the policies of the people's real activities and an indifference on the part of the people toward the formulation of State policies.

"When we look at things in this manner, the fundamental points of the national structure appear clearly: the people should be enabled to take part, from the inside, in the establishing of the country's economic and cultural policies and at the same time these policies should reach all the peripheries of national life. It is only under these conditions that the will and ideas of both those who govern and those who are governed can be fully appreciated by each other and that the total power of the nation can be concentrated on carrying out the policies of the nation.

"A definite national movement is necessary for the successful realization of this national structure. Such a movement should spontaneously spring from the people themselves. If it is planned or guided by the Government, or it is given an administrative structure, it may hinder the spontaneous manifestation of the people's energies. The present circumstances, however, do not allow us to rely only on the spontaneous development of such a movement. Moreover, agitations from below, are liable to degenerate into factional strifes and fail to expand into a really national movement. The Government have thus found it necessary to take positive steps for fostering and directing this movement.

"Viewed in this light, this movement is a common undertaking of both the Government and the people: it is a nation-wide movement to assist the Throne. It is not merely a spiritual movement in the narrow sense but aims at enhancing the political ideals and the political consciousness of the nation. And the choosing of men of talent, known or unknown, from all strata of society to form the nucleus of the movement and thus to obtain a strong political power and driving force is the first and indispensable step that should be taken.

"The movement is highly political in nature, but it is by no means a movement for a political party. Individual and sectional interests and attitudes are necessarily in the very nature of a political party. It is true that there can be no whole without parts; and to condemn parties only because they comprise separate elements is not necessarily fair. It may be said that in those times when liberalism was the basis of economic activities, the existence of political parties was justified. It must be acknowledged that in Japan itself the parties stood up against the influences to make heard the voice of the people. But nevertheless it cannot be denied that the past activities of the parties often were not in keeping with the essential mission of the Diet which is to assist the Throne.

"The new national structure movement aims at superseding the old party politics postulated upon liberalism. It is essentially national, all embracing and public-spirited in character.

"It aims at the concentration and unification of the nation's entire powers. Its activities extend to the whole life of the nation. Even were this movement to rise as a popular movement, its character would not be that of a political party in the old sense. It would on the contrary be a national movement standing above any political party, embracing all parties and factions, economic and cultural bodies, and uniting all in the spirit of public service.

"When such a movement is led by the Government itself, it cannot, in any sense be a party movement. Those who hold the reins of Government and are entrusted with the task of assisting the Throne, are always placed in a position, where they must seek the welfare of the whole but never be permitted to indulge in party politics which, in their very nature, contain elements of sectional antagonism and conflict.

"As I have just stated, the national structure cannot take the form of a political party, especially when it is led by the Government. Neither can it be allowed to take the form of a single party system. This political system takes a 'part' and makes of it a 'whole'; considers the State and the Party as one and the same thing; it views any opposition to the Party as a revolt against the State; it renders permanent the ruling position of one Party with the head of that Party as a permanent wielder of the power to govern. No matter what brilliant results such a system may have reaped in other lands, it is not acceptable in Japan because it is contrary to the basic principle of our national polity of 'One Sovereign over all.' In Japan, it is the privilege of all His Imperial Majesty's subjects to assist the Throne and that privilege cannot be monopolized by the power of either a single individual or a single party.

"If there should arise a difference of opinion concerning the assistance to be offered, the final decision would rest with the Throne. And once an Imperial decision has been given, all the subjects of the Throne should unite in obeying His Majesty's Word. That is the truce essence of Japanese polity.

"In short, the new national structure means a nation-wide and permanent organization in which the Japanese people in all walks of life are to fulfil their duty of assisting the Throne.

"Although the perfection of this structure is by no means an easy task, the Government are convinced that it provided the best means for surmounting the difficulties of these times.

"His Imperial Majesty the Emperor was pleased to grant a message on Februray 11 of this year, showing to His subjects the way in which we should face the present situation. The Government, in obedience to the Imperial Word, are taking the lead on this national movement to assist the Throne. They are resolved to

overcome the great obstacles that confront our country, and to
fulfil the heavy responsibilities which are theirs to guard and
maintain the prosperity of the Imperial Throne."

27 FROM   *John K. Fairbank,*
      Edwin O. Reischauer, Albert M. Craig
          Japan: Fascist or Militarist?

*The authors of the distinguished work from which the next
selection is taken, take strong issue with the view that the Japan
of the late 1930s and early 1940s should be called "fascist." They
prefer the term "militarist." That Japan had no mass party, that
there was no "seizure of power," that its ideology was not very
novel—on these points those who propose and those who oppose
the affixing of the fascist label to Japan agree. The questions that
remain to be settled are (1) was Japan's "Imperial Way" simple
militarism or something more; and (2) if it was something more,
was that something "fascist"?*

THE STRUCTURE OF MILITARIST JAPAN

The rationalization for war came after the outbreak of the
"China Incident." The burden which the limited war in China
placed on the domestic economy was not overwhelming. Yet it
became a pretext for the passage of various laws that little by
little transformed Japan into a militarist state; war became the
national cause in the face of which resistance became impossible.
The opposition of the major parties to the government, which
had typified the stormy period of Hirota and Hayashi cabinets,
vanished almost overnight. War budgets were passed without

SOURCE. John K. Fairbank, Edwin O. Reischauer, and Albert M. Craig,
East Asia: The Modern Transformation, pp. 601–606. Copyright © 1964,
1965 by John K. Fairbank, Edwin O. Reischauer and Albert M. Craig. Copyright © 1960, 1962 by John K. Fairbank and Edwin O. Reischauer. Reprinted
by permission of the publisher, Houghton Mifflin Company.

protest. The Social Mass Party at its November 1937 Congress decided to "positively support the holy war for the fulfillment of the historical mission of the Japanese people." When one Minseitō Diet member protested a national mobilization law as unconstitutional, a lieutenant-colonel told him to shut up. Two years later, when the same man made a speech criticizing the New Order in East Asia, he was expelled from the Diet for having sullied the "holy war." Only five members of the Diet opposed his expulsion, and eight members of the Social Mass Party were expelled from their party for being absent from the Diet when the vote was taken. Long before the parties were formally dissolved in 1940, the Diet had lost its power and become a body which docilely rubber-stamped the decisions of the government.

Power in the government was now in the hands of the cabinet and the services. The Imperial Headquarters was formed in November 1937 to coordinate planning and operations between the two services. The political power of the services was institutionalized in the same month with the inauguration of the Liaison Council which brought together for policy-planning the prime minister, the service ministers, the foreign minister, the army and navy chiefs of staff, and, at times, the home and finance ministers. Council meetings were held during the latter part of 1937 and the early months of 1938. There then occurred a falling-out between the cabinet and the services which lasted until mid-1940. During these two years no meetings were held. They were revived, however, at the time of the second Konoe cabinet in the summer of 1940. After this the Liaison Council became the most important decision-making body in the government. Its most crucial decisions were confirmed at Imperial Conferences.

Economically, the most vital organ of government was the Planning Board established in October 1937 for total national policy formation. Directly under the prime minister, this board planned Japan's wartime economic expansion and administered the controls that were gradually imposed after 1937. Central to its functions were the powers contained in the National Mobilization Law of April 1938, which provided for the control of resources, labor, materials, trade, prices, wages, and services, for censorship of the press and other mass media, and for compulsory registration and savings. This was an enabling act which the Konoe cabinet promised not to use as long as the war remained limited to China. Yet beginning in July 1938, little by little, ordinances were issued putting these controls into effect. Many able men served on the Planning Board. Some had previous experience in the semi-planned economy of Manchuria, some were national-socialists who brought to their work an enthusiasm for planning which overrode their immediate objectives, and some were bright young bureaucrats who had chafed under the seniority system within the other ministries. In 1941 a conflict arose between the Planning Board and the business world. The zaibatsu, while not unwilling to fulfill defense requirements, wished to maintain overall control of their own enterprises within cartelistic associations. They attacked the Planning Board slogan of "public profit first" as Communistic and were able to effect the purge of seventeen leftists from that body. (Some of those arrested at that time, e.g. Wada Hiroo. became prominent in the postwar Socialist Party; some who remained became prominent in the postwar conservative party or in business.) After this incident Lieutenant-General Suzuki became the head of the board, making it more responsive than ever to army influence. And later in 1941 new laws were passed giving it sweeping powers over private enterprise. By the first years of the Pacific war the economy was laced and overlaced with regulations and controls, and was moving largely in response to government direction. In 1943 the Planning Board was absorbed into the new Military Procurement Ministry.

A final aspect of Japan's wartime structure was the national spiritual mobilization movement, also inaugurated after the start of the China war. Directing this movement was the Central Alliance for the Mobilization of the National Spirit, a wrapper-organization which, by the end of 1938, contained 94 lesser organizations—such as the Imperial Veterans Association, the National Mayors Organization, the Japan Labor Unions Council, and so on. The original purpose of the Central Alliance was to coordinate propaganda and promote nationalist and Shintōist activities. As time passed, the alliance took over community defense functions, the sale of war bonds, the collection and distribution of materials, and so on. In October 1940 at the time of the second Konoe cabinet a further advance was made and the Central Alliance was absorbed into the Imperial Rule Assistance Association. This association was patterned after the Nazi "one country, one party" model, and all of Japan's major political parties were dissolved and brought within it. Apparently Konoe hoped at the time of its formation to use it as a counter-weight to the army. However, apart from the negative fact that many other organizations were dissolved in order to form it, it came to very little and totally lacked the dynamism of a political party. Power lay in the government structure, not in the associa-tion, which was no more than a façade plastered over great heterogeneity. The political parties, for example, maintained their factional contentions within its confines. Leadership in the association came into the hands of government leaders: prefec-tural governors became the heads of the prefectural branches. At the lowest level this devolved into neighborhood associations, units of about ten families each, which were also under the effec-tive control of local government offices. These were, at best, an attempt to use the remaining sense of local solidarity to marshal all possible energies for modern total war.

The Nature of Japanese Militarism. Japanese historians have been almost unanimous in terming the changes described above as the growth of fascism in Japan. In part this reflects the con-tinuation of prewar Marxist historiography in postwar Japan, for in Marxist theory a state that is both capitalist and dictatorial can only be fascist. There are, indeed, many critical points of similarity. Both Japan and Germany, for example, moved away from parliamentary government. In both countries a narrow-minded nationalism and the use of terror by a revolutionary right contributed to the rise of authoritarianism. Both abolished the freedoms of speech, press, and assembly; and in both, liberals and leftists who attempted to speak out against aggression or oppressive legislation were persecuted. Both were expansionist, aggressive states. Thus, at a very high level of abstraction it is not impossible to combine these features of Japan and Germany with their common historical character as late modernizers (see page 579) and construct a "fascist model" of political change. Yet, on the whole, the differences between Japan and Germany seem as important as the similarities.

First, their governmental structures were different. Germany had undergone the Weimar change; its government was com-pletely parliamentary and power was in the hands of the domi-nant coalition of parties in the Reichstag. To gain power the Nazis had to obtain a plurality of the votes in a national elec-tion. Japanese government in the 1930's was still at the "pre-

Weimar" stage. As in Germany before World War I, the Diet was only one of several elites. A shift could occur in the character of the government without a shift in the balance of party power in the Diet. Victory at the polls was not a prerequisite for the rise of authoritarian government.

Second, not only was Japanese government in the 1930's more like that in Germany before World War I, but its society was also considerably less "modern" than that of Hitler's Germany. In Germany there was an almost point-to-point correlation between economic change and political polarization. After the runaway inflation of 1922–23 both the Nazis and the Communists rose from very small beginnings to become major parties in the elections of 1924—at the expense of the centrist parties. The economic stabilization achieved by 1928 caused both parties to decline sharply at the polls. Then, under the influence of the world depression both spurted ahead in the early thirties and the numerically superior Nazis maneuvered themselves into power. In this pattern the direct relation between the individual's awareness of his predicament and his reaction to politics at the national level was pathological, not normal. It reflected the breakdown of intermediate institutions—business, welfare, judicial, police (the rise of private armies)—that ordinarily buffered the relation between the individual and the state. The Weimar framework was used to carry out what amounted to direct plebiscites between two extreme, antiparliamentary programs.

In contrast, the traditional (post-1890) social structure was relatively firm in Japan. The two major parties were both centrist, and they were never seriously challenged by an extremist mass party. They continued to get the bulk of the votes, and often the votes went to the more parliamentary of the two. The revolutionary extremist groups that came to prominence in 1931–36 had little influence on the support given to the Seiyūkai and the Minseitō at the polls. And these two parties totally defeated the government-supported, rightist-conservative Shōwa-kai in the 1936 and 1937 elections. The only other tendency visible in the elections of the 1930's was the slow secular trend in favor of semi-liberal socialist parties. Behind the stability in Japanese voting was the fact that intermediate institutions—as in the 1920's —were in good condition. They "contained" the misery of the poorer peasants and workers in the worst years of the depression. The tenant movement was not spurred on but overwhelmed by the coming of the depression, and the rural "community" was re-established—in a somewhat more egalitarian form. The Japanese middle class, such as it was, was also in better shape than its German equivalent. War and inflation wiped out the savings of the middle class in Germany; when the depression came there was nothing for it to fall back on. The Japanese middle class did very well during the war and the 1920's without encountering any serious inflation. The depression hurt small and medium-sized businesses, but bank savings and salaries were worth more than ever. Many remember the early thirties as the "best" period in prewar Japan.

Third, because the government structures and societies were different, the process by which the "antiparliamentary forces" rose was also very different. The Nazis rose as a mass party with a revolutionary program. Taking over the government, the Nazi party remade it in its own image, step by step establishing authoritarian controls. Having created a totalitarian regime, it then made war. Without exaggerating its efficiency, there is no denying its dynamism. But in Japan the antiparliamentary forces were not a dynamic, purposive, united group. It is hard even to describe those who in the 1930's gradually replaced the party leaders in the cabinets, except to say that they were ex-bureaucrats and ex-military men, former members of the Peers and former members of the Privy Council. These men did not plot to seize power. Rather, since the times were not propitious for the parties, nonparty prime ministers were appointed and then more and more nonparty ministers. Behind this "drift" within the establishment were the disputes, maneuvers, and compromises among the multiple elites of government. Communications were often poor and actions uncoordinated. One Japanese scholar has described Japan's path to war as a gradual nervous breakdown within the system. The most dynamic group was the army, which tended to confuse military strategy with national policy. Armies tend to be politically strong in early modernizing states and weak in fully modern states. Japan was not fully modern, and yet its army clearly was not an enlightened counter-elite as in some of the more backward Latin American countries. Rather, within a relatively modern state structure, the power of the Japanese army stemmed from the fact that legally it had never been subordinated to civil control. Its power was exercised within the government organization. By the summer of 1937 Japan was less parliamentary than in 1931, but was not yet totalitarian.

The turning point came when Japan blundered into war with China. The war led to wartime controls. Aiming at the total mobilization of national resources for war, these were sufficiently rigorous by 1941 to be called totalitarian. The official controls were reinforced by community and family pressures of a sort not existing in the West. These demanded not only "right actions" but also "right thoughts," and led to the ethical climate in which university students could be recruited as suicide pilots during the last desperate years of the war. But Japan in this period is better labeled militarist than fascist. The basic state apparatus was not new or revolutionary, but merely the "establishment" overlaid by controls and permeated by an unchecked spiritual nationalism. When the war ended, opinion shifted and the controls were removed, and until the reforms of the Occupation took hold, the basic state structure was much the same as it had been earlier.

Finally, the spiritual difference between Nazi Germany and militarist Japan was immense. In Germany Teutonic myths were used as a vehicle for a value-configuration that would sanction the aggression of the Nazis. Their values were demonic as were their ideas on race, but the myths were never presented as literally true. The problem of reconciling them with natural science did not arise. Rather, the break with the past was a break with the moral position of Christianity, liberalism, and socialism. The enormity of this break necessitated concentration camps and brought about the sense of guilt in the postwar period. In Japan it was not necessary to disinter archaic myths; they were still very much alive and compelled a considerable degree of literal belief. These could be used, almost without change, to justify Japanese expansion. Under the impact of various economic arguments, most people could make the transition from the liberal orthodoxy of the 1920's to the conservative orthodoxy of the 1930's with little sense of a moral break. Many persons were sent to prison, but concentration camps were unnecessary. And after the war, although antimilitarism (the total rejection of the policies of the former leadership) was strong, there was little sense of individual guilt—except in intellectuals' attitudes toward the countries overrun in Asia.

BIBLIOGRAPHICAL NOTE

Fascism has been, since its first appearance, not only a subject for scholarly study but an object of political partisanship. Accounts of fascism have therefore been strongly affected by the political outlook of those who have written about it. It is a striking fact that nearly all serious histories and analyses of fascism have been written by people more or less sharply hostile to it, in contrast to what is the case with communism, where some of the best work has been done by people more or less definitely sympathetic to it. Indeed, the history of the analysis and interpretation of fascism, whose beginnings lie nearly as far back as the beginnings of fascism itself, reflects large-scale shifts in political orientation as much as it reflects the growth of knowledge.

This history may be very roughly divided into three main phases:

1. The first phase, which began soon after 1919 and lasted till 1939 (and beyond), may be called the "socialist" phase. It was largely dominated by a combination of Marxist interpretation and socialist commitment. Some light on this phase is shed by Ernst Nolte, *Three Faces of Fascism*, New York, 1966. The best socialist treatment of fascism stemming from the pre World War II period, and one of the finest analyses of fascism altogether, is A. Rossi (Angelo Tasca), *The Rise of Italian Fascism*, London, 1937. A notable postwar Marxist interpretation is Masao Maruyama, *Thought and Behaviour in Modern Japanese Politics*, London, 1963: see especially the chapter entitled "Fascism—Some Problems." Though Marxist interpretations of fascism are sometimes simplistic, the best of them have the great merit of taking the economic and social bases of fascism seriously, something the works of the second phase conspicuously fail to do.

185

2. The second phase, which may be termed the "cold war" phase, began about 1938 and gained the ascendant in the United States and in Western Europe after 1945. It is characterized by the assimilation of fascism into communism as one of the two facets of what is called "totalitarianism." Fascism as totalitarianism of the right is compared with communism as to totalitarianism of the left, while totalitarianism as a whole is portrayed as somehow the "opposite" (as well as the enemy) of liberal democracy. The best example of cold war "totalitarianism" theory is C. J. Friedrich and Z. Brzezinski, *Totalitarian Dictatorship and Autocracy*, Cambridge, Mass., 1956 and (second edition) 1965. The concept "totalitarianism" is critically analyzed by Alexander J. Groth, "The 'Isms' in Totalitarianism," *American. Political Science Review* 58 (1964), 888–901. Les K. Adler and Thomas G. Paterson have documented the genesis and development of the cold war approach in the United States in "Red Fascism: the Merger of Nazi Germany and Soviet Russia in the American Image of Totalitarianism," *American Historical Review* 75 (1969–1970), 1046–64. They show, *inter alia*, how useful this image was in redirecting hostility from Nazi Germany onto the Soviet Union at the close of World War II. (It is worth noting, parenthetically, that in the same period a parallel cold war maneuver was carried out in the Soviet bloc, where the postwar United States was portrayed as the heir of fascism.) "Totalitarianism" theory focuses on political institutions and on ideology, and has little to say about the social and economic foundations of either fascism or communism. To be sure, the so-called theory of "mass society," which is a corollary of the "totalitarianism" theory, attempts to account for the rise of totalitarianism in terms of the failure of established "elites" and the mobilization of discontented "masses." Whatever the merits of "mass" theory (and I have already suggested in the Introduction that I don't think they are very great), the fact is that the social bases of fascism are so different from those of communism that it is difficult to see how a single simple theory can be adequate to both. In any case, "mass" theory leaves the economic bases wholly out of account. The attendant difficulties for the historian of fascism are recognized, though not solved, by Wolfgang Sauer, "National Socialism: Totalitarianism or Fascism?," *American Historical Review* 73 (1967–1968), 404–24. Serious doubt is cast on the viability of any

theory that simply sees fascism as totalitarianism of the right by both S. M. Lipset, "Fascism—Left, Right and Center," in his book *Political Man*, Garden City, N.Y., 1960, and Hugh Seton-Watson, "Fascism, Left and Right," *Journal of Contemporary History* 1 (1966), 183–197.

3. Neither socialist nor cold war theories are by any means extinct, but a third phase in the interpretation of fascism appears recently to have begun. This third phase reflects the growing interest in the "third world" and in problems of "modernization," and offers some interpretations of fascism in the light of secular processes of social change. Perhaps the most interesting of these is Barrington Moore, Jr., *Social Origins of Dictatorship and Democracy*, Boston, 1966. Moore sees fascism as the price a country may have to pay for not having made a social revolution in the course of modernization, i.e., as a consequence of superimposing a modern capitalist-industrial economy on a premodern social base dominated by agrarian-military ruling classes. It may be significant that Moore's book has far more to say about Japanese fascism than about Italian or German.

* * *

Japan presents a special problem to the student of fascism. Few obvious parallels can be found in Japan either with the rise or the institutions of European fascisms. The inclusion of Japan among countries that went fascist in the interwar period therefore depends on the existence in Japan of phenomena that, though dissimilar in form to those of European fascisms, were similar to them in substance or function. Much interest on this score is to be found in Barrington Moore's book just cited, as well as in Richard Storry, *The Double Patriots: A Study of Japanese Nationalism*, Boston, 1957. The question whether Japan was "really" fascist after 1936 is reopened by G. M. Wilson, "A New Look at the Problem of Japanese Fascism," *Comparative Studies in Society and History* 10 (1967–1968), 401–12, and fresh light is thrown on several facets of the problem by G. M. Wilson., ed., *Crisis in Pre-War Japan*, Tokyo, 1970.

* * *

Limitations of space make it impossible to provide a guide to the vast literature on fascism in its many and varied manifestations. Among general historical treatments of fascism the following recent works will be found useful: Ernst Nolte, *Three Faces of Fascism*, already cited; F. L. Carsten, *The Rise of Fascism*, London, 1967; H. Rogger and E. Weber, eds., *The European Right: A Historical Profile*, Berkeley, Cal., 1965; and the somewhat uneven collections of essays edited by S. J. Woolf, *The Nature of Fascism*, London, 1968, and *European Fascism*, London, 1968. An interesting treatment of fascism as part and parcel of counterrevolutionary politics is provided by Arno Mayer, *Dynamics of Counterrevolution in Europe, 1870–1956*, New York, 1971.